MICHENER'S SOUTH PACIFIC

UNIVERSITY PRESS OF FLORIDA

Florida A&M University, Tallahassee
Florida Atlantic University, Boca Raton
Florida Gulf Coast University, Ft. Myers
Florida International University, Miami
Florida State University, Tallahassee
New College of Florida, Sarasota
University of Central Florida, Orlando
University of Florida, Gainesville
University of North Florida, Jacksonville
University of South Florida, Tampa
University of West Florida, Pensacola

Michener's
South Pacific

STEPHEN J. MAY

University Press of Florida

Gainesville

Tallahassee

Tampa

Boca Raton

Pensacola

Orlando

Miami

Jacksonville

Ft. Myers

Sarasota

Copyright 2011 by Stephen J. May
Printed in the United States of America. This book is printed on Glatfelter
Natures Book, a paper certified under the standards of the Forestry
Stewardship Council (FSC). It is a recycled stock that contains 30 percent
post-consumer waste and is acid-free.

16   15   14   13   12   11   6   5   4   3   2   1

Library of Congress Cataloging-in-Publication Data
May, Stephen J. (Stephen James), 1946-
Michener's South Pacific / Stephen J. May.
p. cm.
Includes bibliographical references and index.
ISBN 978-0-8130-3557-4 (alk. paper)
1. Michener, James A. (James Albert), 1907–1997. Tales of the South Pacific.
2. Michener, James A. (James Albert), 1907–1997—Knowledge—Oceania.
3. Michener, James A. (James Albert), 1907–1997—Travel—Oceania. 4. World
War, 1939–1945—Personal narratives, American. 5. World War, 1914–1918—
United States—Literature and the war. 6. Oceania—In literature. I. Title.
PS3525.I19T353 2011
813.'54—dc22   2010031998

The University Press of Florida is the scholarly publishing agency for the
State University System of Florida, comprising Florida A&M University,
Florida Atlantic University, Florida Gulf Coast University, Florida
International University, Florida State University, New College of Florida,
University of Central Florida, University of Florida, University of North
Florida, University of South Florida, and University of West Florida.

University Press of Florida
15 Northwest 15th Street
Gainesville, FL 32611-2079
http://www.upf.com

FOR THOSE WHO SERVED

Contents

Preface ix

Prologue xi

PART I. THE PATHS OF THE SEA

  1. The Mutiny 3

  2. Espíritu Santo 13

  3. Nesomaniac 26

  4. Two Tales 36

  5. Tontouta 43

  6. *Tales of the South Pacific* 53

PART II. ON BROADWAY

  7. Coming Home 63

  8. "An Ugly, Monstrous Book" 73

  9. A Kid from Doylestown 79

10. The Prize 87

11. Mary and Ezio 92

12. Josh and Oscar 98

13. Those Enchanted Evenings 106

PART III. RETURN TO PARADISE

14. Island Hopping 115

15. The Man from Palau 127

16. Hawaii Mon Amour   132
17. Misadventures in Paradise   144
18. Lord Jim   151

Acknowledgments   161
Notes   163
Bibliography   171
Index   173

Preface

James A. Michener (1907–1997) is widely considered one of America's premier storytellers. In a career that spanned five decades, he pioneered the sociohistorical novel and provided us profound glimpses of foreign cultures. With such highly detailed and intensely researched works as *Hawaii*, *Iberia*, *The Source*, *Centennial*, *Chesapeake*, and *Poland*, he enriched the minds of generations and, in the process, dominated the best-seller lists for many years. Winner of the Pulitzer Prize, recipient of the Presidential Medal of Freedom and more than twenty honorary doctorates of letters, he was a true fixture in American literature.

But no part of Michener's distinguished career is more compelling than its beginning, in those dark war years when his fledgling talent took wing. If someone were to write a script depicting a successful writer, I can think of no one's story more powerful and dramatic than Michener's. This is the story of those years, a period marked by war, separation, loneliness, and adventure, when the prospect of a writing career seemed as remote as the Pacific islands themselves.

His initial success came in 1947 with the publication of *Tales of the South Pacific*, which went on to win the Pulitzer Prize and the approval of several of America's major critics. It also became the darling of Joshua Logan, Richard Rodgers, and Oscar Hammerstein, who transformed Michener's *Tales* into the smash Broadway musical *South Pacific*. The play won its own Pulitzer Prize and continued over the decades to thrill and enchant audiences both in America and around the world. In the spring of 2008, the play was revived at the Vivian Beaumont Theater at Lincoln

Center. Critics swooned over this production, which won seven Tony awards. As of this writing it is still playing in New York and on the road. Michener's exotic island of Bali Ha'i has become perhaps the most famous fictional island in literature. And today his experiences with war, racial intolerance, and forbidden love seem never more pertinent.

The idea for this book came quite suddenly and was perhaps prompted by the lack of a serious study of Michener's war years that ultimately led to his first work, *Tales of the South Pacific*, and the later success of *South Pacific*. A few years ago I was invited to be part of the fiftieth anniversary edition of the movie version of *South Pacific*. We did several filmed interviews at the William Fox Theater, a venerable old place steeped in movie history, on the Fox lot in Hollywood. The theater had seen the screenings of many movies over the years, and I thought at any moment the ghosts of Henry Fonda, Betty Grable, and Darryl F. Zanuck might saunter down the aisle, cigarettes dangling from their lips, eyeing me with suspicion.

During the taping, accomplished over a few days, several of us, including producer Steven Smith, film critic Jon Burlingame, and the star of the movie *South Pacific*, Mitzi Gaynor, were sitting around, off camera, discussing the merits of Michener's book, the Broadway musical, and the film. They asked me several questions about Michener and the war he wrote so vividly about. As I tried to answer them, it became apparent to me that there was a lot I didn't know about Michener's war and postwar years that other people might be interested in as well. On the plane returning home, I began to formulate how this study of Michener's career would take shape and the research I would need in order to complete it. From that moment on, the words fell into place.

Prologue

When the attack on Pearl Harbor drew the United States into the war in December 1941, James A. Michener was an industrious and ambitious textbook editor at Macmillan Publishing in New York City. Although he had been with the company less than a year, he seemed to be well on his way to moving up the ladder. At thirty-three years of age, he possessed all the qualities of scholarship, intelligence, and drive that made an ideal employee. Underneath his outward demeanor, however, lurked the heart of a maverick. This rebellious side of Michener would ultimately lead him out of the textbook business and into the world of literature.

Raised as a Quaker, he immediately thought that he could declare himself a conscientious objector. Yet the more he probed his patriotism and his desire to serve his country, the more he became dedicated to seeking a commission in the army. As other Macmillan employees lined up for military service and the ranks thinned, his dedication increased. At the time he was married to a woman whom had he met in the mid-1930s and who was currently serving with Eisenhower's army in Europe. Their marriage was never a strong one. The months dragged on with no word of an officer's commission for Michener. The battle of the Coral Sea raged in the South Pacific in May 1942, and then in August the ferocious battle for Guadalcanal began. Meanwhile Michener waited, editing his books.

Then in early 1943 a commission in the United States Navy was approved. At first Michener was kept stateside, performing clerical duties with the Bureau of Aeronautics in Washington, D.C. Later that year he was transferred to the Aviation Supply Depot in Philadelphia. He petitioned his superiors for a better assignment, and by January 1944 he was sure that he would be sent to the Mediterranean, whose waters he had sailed in the early 1930s as a chart boy for the British merchant marine. The navy considered his request but eventually turned him down. More critical then were the conflicts in the South Pacific. Michener raised a rather timid protest to his superiors, saying that he was more qualified for the European theater of war. In the end they ordered him to report to San Francisco, where he would ship out for the South Pacific.

He returned briefly to New York to settle some business matters. He then cleaned out his Greenwich Village brownstone, packed his bags, said farewell to his Macmillan friends, and boarded the train for the West Coast. In his naval uniform at bustling Penn Station, his trench coat draped over his arm, Michener looked like any other sailor or marine headed overseas. Unknown to him was that the war he was heading for would ultimately redefine his career, his worldview, and everything he held dear.

When he arrived in San Francisco, he headed for the harbor and gazed upon the troopship that would carry him to his duty station in the South Pacific. It was not an inspiring sight.

PART I

The Paths of the Sea

CHAPTER 1

The Mutiny

Everyone agreed: the transport *Cape Victory* was the ugliest ship in the navy. Its chipped paint was a seasick gray, its shape suggested a crumpled cigar, and its quarters were dark and labyrinthine. Its civilian crew was even more infamous. The captain, who rarely if ever consulted with anyone, ran his ship with Ahabian discipline. The rest of the crew went about their business with steadfast and obedient silence. Requisitioned by the navy soon after the start of the war, the *Cape Victory* joined other transport ships in carrying soldiers, sailors, and marines to military bases in the South Pacific. With only one gun forward and lacking an escort cruiser, it made an easy target for Japanese aircraft.

In the spring of 1944 the South Pacific remained a vicious battleground, where the Japanese were determined to thrust further toward Australia, and the Americans and Allies were determined to repulse them. The Solomon Islands, just east of New Guinea, stood in the way of Japanese ambitions. In August of 1942 the Americans won a decisive battle on Guadalcanal, one of the most strategic islands in the Solomon chain. By April of the following year, the American and Japanese navies were still fighting for permanent control of the islands. To this end the Americans were pouring fresh detachments of men into the island base of Espíritu Santo, the major staging area for assaults on the Solomons and surrounding island chains in jeopardy of enemy invasion. Santo, as it was affectionately called, was one of the destinations of the *Cape Victory* and would be the home of Lieutenant (Junior Grade) James Michener for the next year and a half.

"Man the Guns" poster, 1942.
Courtesy National Archives.

Three days out of San Francisco, Michener was still getting accustomed to the dull throb of the engines and the endless blue sweep of the Pacific. To pass the time, he lounged on the aft deck, read, and watched the waves tower and crest in the distance. Other times he went below-decks and swapped stories with his newfound friends. One of them was a seasoned veteran named Lieutenant Richmond, a loquacious man of action who had managed his own construction company and now was a proud member of the Seabees—the famous "can do" navy battalions that quickly built airstrips, bulldozed roads, and built bridges. Richmond had the uncanny ability to transfer his cigarette from one corner of his mouth to the other simply by using his tongue. He was probably the inspiration for Tony Fry, the roguish wheeler-dealer of *South Pacific* fame. Richmond entertained Michener with his stories of Middle America. Michener had spent a few years teaching prep school and then lectured for a few years at the University of Northern Colorado and at Harvard. Bookish and intellectual, in civilian life usually sporting a bow tie, he looked like a scholar you might find poking around a library.

Lieutenant Junior Grade James A. Michener in naval uniform, before shipping out to the South Pacific, 1943. Courtesy Library of Congress.

One memorable conversation between the two revolved around their anticipated duty. Michener told Richmond he was headed to Espíritu Santo. Richmond said he was getting off at Guadalcanal.

It was well known that Guadalcanal was still in the thick of the fighting, while Santo was away from most of the action in the South Pacific. Richmond explained that his navy job was beachmaster, a kind of choreographer for a seaborne invasion: "When there's an amphibious landing, the admiral in charge commands while the troops are aboard his ships, the general when they're on land. We've found at all the major landings that there's a fearfully critical period when things are piling up on the beach: men, mobile guns, supplies, the whole crap of modern warfare. In those crucial minutes between the admiral letting go and the general taking over, the beachmaster takes charge."

"Sounds like a pretty dangerous job," said Michener.

"The tough ones, who know what they're doing, they never let control slip away," Richmond said, and added evenly, "No one is going to take my beach away from me. No one."

Compared to Richmond's duties, Michener's sounded tame.

"I'm to visit all the Navy air units to be sure they have the necessary manuals for the operation and maintenance of our airplanes, especially those on our carriers." Michener admitted he was a paper pusher, but said he would be studying secret reports so that he could impress on pilots "the structural limits of their planes. How fast and deep they can fly before their wings fall off."

•

Aboard the *Cape Victory*, unrest brewed. There was a clear division between the navy contingent and the civilian personnel running the ship. Captain Bossard, the civilian skipper, never appeared on deck, but his orders were regularly relayed. At the beginning of the voyage, a bullhorn bellowed: "Now hear this! In order not to leave a detectable trail floating on the sea for a Jap submarine to latch onto and track us down, you will throw nothing, I repeat nothing, overboard, night or day. If you are caught doing so, it's into the brig on bread and water. And if it looks to us as if you had been doing it on purpose to leave such a trail, you will be shot." The men were also warned not to loiter around the protective railing circling the ship. "Because I promise you," the voice intoned, "that if you fall overboard . . . we will not stop or double back to pick you up."

Sneering at this raffish collection of recruits, the captain remained in his quarters for the whole trip. So did the army colonel who was supposedly in charge of the military transferees. It was rumored that the pair passed most of the voyage drinking.

At mess one evening Richmond growled: "Lieutenant, is this food as god-awful as I think it is?"

"Worse," said Jim.

Together they took stock of their miserable daily menu: rancid bacon, leathery pancakes, cold coffee, tasteless bread. Even more infuriating was the knowledge that the crew were, at *their* table, enjoying mouth-watering cuts of meat, piping hot coffee, and fresh eggs. Richmond, Michener, and several fellow officers agreed that something had to be done. While their buddies worked on a list of grievances, Richmond and Jim took action.

Together they headed down to the refrigerated lockers where provisions were stored. With the aid of Richmond's pistol, they were able to get a look inside. The mess crew admitted that union rules guaranteed the crew sumptuous meals, while the military rated no such attention. Richmond and Michener found a quite corner of the ship and considered their next move.

Both, of course, were painfully aware of possible repercussions. Michener said: "From what I've read about ships at sea, let alone the formal Navy, it's pretty dangerous for anyone to start trouble. Mutiny and all that. The rules are quite stringent."

"But isn't it obvious, Prof, that our government is paying this ship to transport us in reasonably decent style and that someone is taking that money and slipping it into his pocket?"

Jim reminded him about the union rules dictating that a crew be fed properly.

Richmond shot back: "Damn it all, we saw enough food down there to feed an army. We could *all* be eating the way those others do."

In addition to the poor food, there was growing anger among the recruits over water rationing. Michener jotted down their grievances. Then he and Richmond stormed up to the captain's quarters to present their list to the highest authorities on the ship. Richmond knocked on the door and voiced their concerns. There was no response. "We stood around for a while," Michener later wrote, "looking silly, then backed off and never did confront the scoundrels."

Still fuming, the two headed back to the lockers in the galley. Telling themselves, "Hell, if they want us to run the ship our way, we'll do it," they ordered the cooks to open the doors. While Michener stood guard, Richmond unloaded an abundant supply of meats and produce, plus flour for biscuits and pancakes. Lieutenant Michener then ordered the cooks to prepare a decent meal for the military as well as the crew. This scene was quietly repeated daily. At night, staring at the human lump in the bunk above him, Jim mused about the whole affair. Why did the captain and crew not react to their mutiny? From many possibilities, Michener decided that "if they were to arrest us and invoke a court-martial, they would be involved in months of unpleasantness that would have to reveal their mismanagement, so it was wiser to let things slide." The voyage would soon be over, and he and Richmond and their fellow passengers would enter the hell of war. In Michener's mind, justice had been served.

Years afterwards, Michener reflected on his actions: "When a basic principle was involved . . . I would dig in, and long after others had sur-rendered the fight I would still be there flailing away. . . . I did not surrender easily, but that characteristic . . . was not a sign of my moral courage; it was more an innate desire to see the thing that someone else might have started brought to a sensible conclusion."

•

As the *Cape Victory* neared the equator, the Pacific war was entering its most grueling and dangerous phase. Just five months before, American forces, in an assault code-named Operation Galvanic, had stormed ashore on Tarawa Atoll in the Gilbert Islands. As part of the "island hopping" campaign to painstakingly retake control of the area, the battle was the second time that the Americans had been on the offensive (the battle for

Guadalcanal being the first). Tarawa was particularly crucial because it lay on a strategic route to retake the Philippines. Wading through water under withering gunfire, the marines of the Second Division had arduously made their way ashore. The 4,500 Japanese defenders fought virtually to the last man. Short in duration compared to Guadalcanal, but violent in its intensity, the battle tested every aspect of a successful amphibious landing.

On the *Cape Victory* rumors spread rapidly. The most persistent one involved the next major operation, which was said to include the invasion of Saipan, in the Marianas, slated for the summer of 1944. Michener contemplated how he might be drawn into the action. At first his military assignment was purely behind the lines, but he was not reticent about volunteering for greater duties. Aiding his maneuvering for duty in the Pacific was the perception by many officers aboard the *Cape Victory* that he was related to Vice Admiral Marc A. Mitscher, the renowned commander of the Fast Carrier Task Force involved in actions in the Solomons and the Philippines. When the middle syllable of "Michener" is elided or slurred, the names sound very similar. Although there was no connection between the two men, Lieutenant Michener let people assume such a relation existed. Even after he left the *Cape Victory* and traveled throughout the South Pacific during the remaining months of the war, Michener enjoyed the benefits of this name confusion.

In addition to an aroused sense of justice, James Michener brought a self-assurance to his military role. Born in New York City on February 3, 1907, he came to live with Mabel Michener, a single mother, in Doylestown, Pennsylvania, as her adopted son, even though there is strong evidence that she was in fact his birth mother. There he grew up as a member of Mabel's rambunctious houseful of abandoned children. At one time, twelve other children lived under the same roof with Jim and his mother.

Neighbors called the Michener home "a madhouse with children running everywhere." For young Jim, it was a hardscrabble childhood. Disease, malnutrition, and the threat of eviction stalked their existence. Mabel and the children ended up moving from house to house in Doylestown, while she carved out a meager living as a seamstress.

In the midst of sheer deprivation, the naturally introspective young Jim fashioned personal happiness when he withdrew into a world of art, music, and literature. His uncle Arthur introduced him to opera, a passion he was to follow throughout his life. Always alive to visual beauty, Jim stuffed an old shoebox with landscape paintings that he cut out of discarded magazines. He studied poetry and devoured novels, particularly those of Balzac, Tolstoy, and Dickens. In short, he became a school of one, believing that he could educate himself and thereby arm himself for success.

When times got too difficult for Mabel Michener, she often sent Jim to the poorhouse south of Doylestown, which was managed by the husband of her sister Hannah. Here Jim received an education in human misery that stimulated him as a burgeoning writer, kindled his imagination, and seared his memory. Throughout his later life, he reflected on his time spent among the elderly and impoverished men and women who lived out their final days in the Doylestown poorhouse. "I made up my mind in that poorhouse," he noted, "that I would do anything, *anything* to keep myself out of there. These were pathetic people whose lives had soured, and I was not going to end up on the same ash heap."

Despite his poorhouse experience, Michener loved growing up in Bucks County, Pennsylvania. With its leafy sanctuaries, fenceless meadows, honking motorcars, and Henry Chapman Mercer's ornate castles dotting the landscape, the area was rich in natural beauty and tradition.

In his teens Michener became a shabby vagabond and traveled by thumb and rail across America, once heading as far west as Wyoming before the age of seventeen. He worked for the Burpee Seed Company growing and picking phlox for several summers and also toiled on an asparagus farm. While attending Doylestown High School in the early 1920s, he worked summers in the Willow Grove amusement park, where he met such musical masters as Victor Herbert and John Philip Sousa.

In 1925 Michener received a scholarship to prestigious Swarthmore College near Philadelphia. Although he did not write with any success while at college, he read and studied voraciously, nurturing in the process what he referred to as his "bear trap memory." In his four years at Swarthmore, he memorized more than two hundred poems and developed his intellect into a formidable weapon in the classroom.

After graduation from Swarthmore in 1929, he taught at the Hill School near Pottstown, Pennsylvania, and later at the George School in Newtown. In 1935, at the age of twenty-eight, Michener married Patti Koon, the daughter of a Lutheran minister from South Carolina. Described as "ostentatiously unfeminine," she enjoyed playing sports such as baseball and tennis. In temperament, intellect, and physical appearance, she was exactly the opposite of Jim. "Patti was actually a very dear person," a friend commented. "She just had no feminine ways. She was happy-go-lucky and full of fun. She and Jim got along fine, although they were not what you would call close." This sense of dislocation and separation characterized their thirteen-year marriage, some of which, because of the war, was spent apart. Patti followed him to a college teaching job in Colorado in 1936; in 1939 she went with him to Harvard University, where he began a visiting professorship in social studies.

When the war came and Jim seemed mired in his job at Macmillan Publishing, Patti joined the army and was sent to Europe. She managed to write only three or four letters to Michener while they were apart.

He voyaged to the war-torn South Pacific virtually without any strong relationships from which to draw solace. But that's how James Michener lived his life: vicariously and passionately—and very much a free spirit.

Michener on the deck of the *Cape Victory*, bound for Espíritu Santo, 1944. Courtesy Library of Congress.

One of the most exciting events on board the *Cape Victory* proved to be the crossing of the equator. "Crossing the line," as it was known in nautical circles, involved the initiation of greenhorn sailors, or "polliwogs," by the veterans of the equator crossing, called "shellbacks." During the ceremony, which could last one to two days, enlisted men were allowed to badger their officer superiors. "Wogs" were humiliated and derisively labeled benchwarmers, landlubbers, draft dodgers, lounge lawyers, squaw men, sand crabs, sodbusters, beachcombers, and any other name that seemed appropriate. While other initiation rites marked the passing of the international dateline and the circling of the globe, the equator crossing was one of the more famous—or infamous, if you were a "wog." Polliwogs like Michener were treated to good-natured ribbing and mildly abusive hazing such as being called "a four-eyed hack" and sprayed with a can of shaving cream. Wogs who were not so lucky were made to crawl on hands and knees through chutes of rotting garbage or coerced into dressing in swimsuit drag and parading in front of their shipmates. Other ships had more extreme forms of hazing, such as blasting initiates down a canvas chute with a fire hose. The ceremony was reigned over by King Neptune and his court, usually composed of shellbacks returning for their second or third tours of duty, who passed judgment on the various "wogs" and deemed them suitable to enter the vast and fabled kingdom of the South Pacific.

After crossing the line, the polliwogs received their certificates of equatorial baptism, which included the passage "Should he fall overboard, we do command that all sharks, dolphins, whales, mermaids and other dwellers in the deep are to abstain from maltreating his person." A more coveted honor for any mariner was to be distinguished as a golden shellback, which meant that he had crossed into Neptune's kingdom at the exact point where the equator intersects the international dateline. Owing to Japanese ship movements in the region, however, the *Cape Victory* set a course far south of this point.

The days dragged on. On deck Michener might join the throngs of sailors playing cards or writing letters home. Mostly he sat by himself in a folding chair brought from belowdecks, reading or soaking up the sun, his eyelids heavy and languid. The sun blazed on the shimmering immensity of blue. The whitecaps raced by. An orphaned cloud wandered aimlessly overhead. Under these circumstances it was hard to believe that war loomed on the horizon, that navy guns were mercilessly shelling some pristine beach, or that scores of dead marines were bobbing in the surf of some scorched and blasted atoll. It was hard to imagine there was such a thing as war. The lordly sun, the briny air, the near absolute serenity of all things under heaven proclaimed otherwise.

But it could not last.

Espíritu Santo

In 1940 Espíritu Santo was a drowsy, enchanted Pacific island where the loudest noise was the daily scouring of the beaches by the waves. Towering palm trees nodded and rustled in the balmy tropic breezes. Tranquil, sun-drenched days dwindled into indigo nights radiant with stars. As the largest island in the New Hebrides chain, it supported a modest population of indigenous peoples, expatriate European planters, and a force of Tonkinese laborers. Within three years, Santo was transformed into a bustling naval base overrun with jeeps, antiaircraft guns, and swarms of Seabees. At one time or another, 45,000 servicemen called the island a temporary home. An airstrip had been hacked out of the jungle just north of the harbor at Luganville. As the Japanese drove deeper into Melanesia and continuously threatened the nearby Solomon Islands, Santo became a fortress of men and materiel.

The south-facing harbor had also changed drastically. Instead of a scattering of native canoes, an armada of nearly one hundred ships—cruisers, destroyers, and transports—lay at anchor. Michener attributed Santo's careful selection to Admiral John S. "Slew" McCain, the grandfather of Arizona senator and 2008 presidential candidate John McCain. Admiral McCain, who commanded all land-based air operations for the invasion of Guadalcanal, had scouted the New Hebrides after the Japanese attack on Pearl Harbor. Flying low over Santo's natural harbor, he pointed down and exclaimed: "That's where we'll build our base." Shortly thereafter, the Seabees landed and fired up their bulldozers.

The Seabees of the Third Construction Battalion, who according to one army officer "smelled like goats, lived like dogs and worked like horses," were dispersed throughout Santo and quickly built the airstrip, which was followed by the installation of drainage pipes, fuel tanks, supply depots, washing machines, and ice cream freezers. Within a few short months the Seabees had transformed a primitive island into one of the most tactically advanced bases in the world.

The navy soon controlled all communications in and out of the island. Navy censors scrupulously pored over a sailor's mail, redacting any portions that revealed his duty station. As the war went along, however, sailors found creative ways to send coded messages to alert their loved ones back home as to their whereabouts. One method was to write out the sailor's name using a different middle initial in each successive letter. For example, Michener might use this code in five consecutive letters:

James S. Michener
James A. Michener
James N. Michener
James T. Michener
James O. Michener

The letters' recipient would deduce that the writer was on Espíritu Santo in the New Hebrides. Overworked junior officers, who usually served as the censors, would often not recognize the deception.

Disembarking from the *Cape Victory* in late April 1944, Michener and several other servicemen reported to the billets on the naval base near the harbor. Michener was assigned to one of the Quonset huts erected in rows thirty feet apart. He was also assigned a jeep for transportation around the island, as well as two corpsmen to serve as his couriers. Among other items, the navy provided him with a bulky typewriter. Several of the keys stuck, so he often had to hammer them with force. He never mastered the technique of using all his fingers on the keyboard; instead he relied on his two index fingers to hunt and peck his way through a report.

His Quonset faced the drab corrugated façades of its neighbors. Platoons of nameless sailors came and went. He made friends with his nearest neighbor, a man identified by Michener only as Fred, who made primitive shell necklaces by stuffing cowries with a mixture of cotton and aviation glue. A line of eager servicemen was usually lined up in front of Fred's

Michener in South Pacific officers' casual dress, 1944. Courtesy Library of Congress.

door when a sale was announced. Michener admired his industriousness, for, unlike like many servicemen on Santo, Fred had found a way to deal with the interminable boredom. "Our war was waiting," observed Michener. "You rotted on New Caledonia waiting for Guadalcanal. Then you sweated twenty pounds away in Guadal waiting for Bougainville. There were battles, of course. But they were flaming things of the bitter moment. A blinding flash at Tulagi. A day of horror at Tarawa. . . . Then you relaxed and waited. And pretty soon you hated the man next to you, and you dreaded the look of a coconut tree."

It was the lassitude, much more than the actual battle, that took the greatest toll on the human psyche. Over time men dealt with it in either positive or negative ways. Some sought solace in groups of other men who discussed their civilian lives or the fear of battle; some went to the movies, or read books from the library; some could not deal with the waiting. A sailor from a Quonset hut near Michener's was found dangling from a coconut tree; another swam out into the harbor and was never heard from again. They guzzled torpedo juice—and if the ethyl alcohol did not kill them outright, a slower, more painful death awaited them.

Marines storm Tarawa, 1943. Operation Galvanic to assault Tarawa Atoll inspired Operation Alligator in Michener's *Tales of the South Pacific*. Courtesy National Archives.

For Michener, who had his own bouts of inactivity and depression, island living presented great opportunities. Always the explorer and student of different cultures, he frequently left the base and journeyed on foot or by jeep to various parts of Santo. The navy base and harbor occupied the southeastern tip of the island. The western portion, ringed by volcanic headlands, was mostly impenetrable jungle. The eastern coastline was ragged and uncharted, offering few if any anchorages. In the heart of Santo, native people carried on an existence virtually untouched by civilization. Near the harbor several European—mainly French—expatriates cultivated their copra and coffee plantations, which were worked by Tonkinese laborers imported from what is now Vietnam. The "Tonks" offered cheap labor, fulfilling their duties with near steadfast devotion. Most of them were indentured to their planters, who fed, clothed, and housed them, with the view that they would be returned to their homeland when their service time was completed.

Michener came to love the sounds of the tropics. Two of the more audible features were the wind rushing through the coconut palms and the torrent of noise emanating from the night jungle. In calm weather the roof of palm fronds moved fluidly, the tenuous quiver of the leaves stopped only by a sudden lull in the breeze. Throughout the day the palms heaved, sighed, and moaned. When a gale was imminent, however, the palms would twitter and giggle above the incessant rumble of jeeps and ambulances. As the storm bore down, the palms sobbed and thrashed. The noise would gather and swell to fever pitch. Then the rain came. Huge sheets of water drenched the island for days. When the rain stopped, the wind slackened and the great liquid forest returned to its soft irregular breathing. At night the jungle outside Michener's Quonset came alive. While he typed his reports late into the night, the cry of herons and shriek of crickets haunted him.

The indigenous tribes of Santo ignored the military for the most part and retained a near–Stone Age existence. They grew avocados and melons, but preferred the taste of taro, yam, and especially pigs. They walked naked or half naked through the jungles, and at night they sat down and told their favorite Creation stories. They drank kava, a bitter concoction made from the roots of *Piper methysticum*, which produces lightheadedness and volubility. The stories always involved their ancestors, who had emerged at the dawn of time from the very heart of Santo. They had grown from live creatures or from trees. They had not migrated here from other islands, and there was never a mention of ships or long voyages during the revelation of their past.

Cannibalism, once a tradition in the New Hebrides, had recently died out. But the Seabees still heard talk of it lingering in the dark valleys of Santo. Cannibal stories were rife on the base. "Better not head into the hinterland or you'll end up in the pot, and they'll have your shrunken head up on a pole in the village," the navy veterans would say. Over the years, the Melanesian peoples retained a special fondness for the taste of human flesh, called "long pig." Now, however, instead of finding a stray missionary or a wandering GI, they settled for canned meat or corned beef, which they claimed ran a close second in the taste department.

While many of the indigenous people isolated themselves from the military, some praised the Americans and their wonderful technology. Called "cargo cults," these natives worshipped the cargoes of American goods which they believed were destined for them by their ancestors. Many of them had never before seen an airplane, a radio, a navy cruiser, or such an amazing device as an electric razor. They watched wide-eyed as the navy offloaded a storehouse of wondrous material goods. Employing a form of sympathetic magic that imitated the practices of their occupiers, the islanders carved headphones from wood, built mock airstrips, lit torches to illuminate the runways, staged marching drills with stick rifles, and painted their bodies with navy insignias, believing that the Americans (or the Japanese, as the case may be) possessed some mysterious connection to deities and to their ancestors. Cargo cults flourished especially around the port town of Luganville, where knots of natives hung out, crying wildly as each jeep or staff car drove by.

One of Michener's favorite drives on Santo followed the eastern shoreline for a few miles until it dead-ended halfway up the coast. He would park his jeep and take in the cobalt sweep of sea. To the northeast, perhaps sixteen miles away, he could distinguish a mysterious volcanic atoll rising like a pyramid through the mist. This was Aoba, sometimes called Oba or Omba or Ambae. Although he ventured there only on one occasion, toward the end of 1944, it remained a compelling reminder that the South Pacific was still a place far removed from war, trauma, and misery.

Was Aoba the fabled island of Bali Ha'i in Michener's first work of fiction? Most certainly it was. In Michener's book, however, there are two islands, side by side. Michener described Bali Ha'i as appearing out of the mists behind a larger island, Vanicoro. "Bali-ha'i was an island of the sea, a jewel of the vast ocean. It was small. Like a jewel, it could be perceived in one loving glance. . . . It was green like something ever youthful, and it seemed to curve itself like a woman into the rough shadows formed by the volcanoes on the greater island of Vanicoro." He describes the imaginary Vanicoro as "a large and brooding island, miasmic with malaria, old fetishes, sickness and deep shadows." Why would Michener create two islands when, geographically speaking, there was only one?

Perhaps the answer lies in a brief excursion Michener made to Mono Island in the Treasury Islands during a mopping-up operation after the Japanese departed. He jotted down in a notebook a name scrawled on a sign near an abandoned village: "Bali Ha'i." After returning to Santo, he mentioned the name to one of the natives, who offered him a rough translation: "Balai-hai" means "one of a pair." The name was certainly more musical and enchanting than Aoba, and perhaps Michener felt compelled to follow through on the literal meaning of the term. By employing it in his stories, he would make the two islands more strongly symbolize the mother-daughter relationship of Bloody Mary and Liat.

Aubert Ratard had arrived in Santo from France in the 1920s and, like so many who left their native countries, was unwilling to divulge the exact reasons for his expatriation. In the nineteenth century the great European powers—principally Great Britain, Germany, the Netherlands, and France—colonized large portions of the South Pacific and then spent agonizing years trying to unload them. France retained colonies in French Polynesia, New Caledonia, and the New Hebrides. When Ratard arrived, he immediately began developing his copra plantation into one of the most successful on Santo. Throughout the 1930s he expanded production and imported increasingly more Tonkinese laborers to meet his goals.

In 1940, when France fell to Nazi Germany, two factions developed to cope with the occupation. The first, commanded by Marshal Pétain, transferred power to the Germans and for the most part surrendered French will in turn; the second, commanded by General Charles de Gaulle, formed the movement known as the Free French, which vowed to fight on and continue resistance until France freed herself or was liberated by the Allies. The Free French movement soon spread to colonies around the world, including the New Hebrides, where Ratard became its de facto leader. "He was in his middle forties," Michener wrote, "slim, a bit stoop-shouldered. His eyes were black and deep-set. . . . He had long arms and wrists, and although he used his hands constantly in making conversation, they were relaxed and delicate in their movements." Delicacy, however, figured little in Ratard's determination to foil the Japanese or to rid his island of American troops.

When the threat of invasion by the Japanese diminished and the Americans instead erected their rear-echelon base in Luganville, Ratard became something of a folk hero. Commanders sought his knowledge of the New Hebrides and Solomon Islands. Lieutenant Michener was dispatched to Ratard's plantation principally to form a bond of friendship between the Americans and the Frenchman and to elicit any important information that he could.

Through the summer and fall of 1944, Jim visited Ratard and his family more than twenty times. His plantation stood on a ridge near the harbor, ringed in coconut palms and possessing stunning views of the ocean. Fifty or so workers' huts were scattered on the property. One hut, erected a short distance from the others, was occupied by Ratard's father, who was afflicted with leprosy. Ratard cared for him and ensured he got the most modern medical assistance. Soon Michener became less a military inquisitor and more an amiable friend. On these dinner visits, he was usually cornered by the plantation's spokesperson, the irrepressible Tonkinese woman known as Bloody Mary. Half purring kitten and half wild boar, she filled Michener's ear with her complaints, usually spiced with some lusty GI profanity. When he made her a character in *Tales of the South Pacific*, he described her this way:

> She was, I judge, about fifty-five. She was not more than five feet tall, weighed about 110 pounds, had few teeth and those funereally black, was sloppy in dress, and had thin ravines running out from the corners of her mouth. These ravines, about four on each side, were usually filled with betel juice, which made her look as if her mouth had been gashed with a rusty razor. Her name, Bloody Mary, was well given.

Bloody Mary and the other Tonkinese laborers had a quarrel not with Monsieur Ratard but with the French colonial government in Port-Vila, capital of the New Hebrides, on the neighboring island of Efate, or Vaté. When war came, the French authorities prevented the Tonkinese from returning to their homeland. Fearing that the plantations would be abandoned, they set down an edict that any repatriation would not happen until the war in the Pacific ended. Bloody Mary put it bluntly: "War come. Three years finish. No go home. Four years, five years, no damn good." Most indenture agreements between the French and the Tonkinese had been made several years before the war. These had lapsed long since, and the Tonkinese were retained against their will.

Bloody Mary told Michener that after the war was over she would return to Tonkin and oppose French colonialism. "I would often think of her in later years," remarked Michener, "when American troops were fighting their fruitless battles in Vietnam and I wondered if our leaders realized that the enemy they were fighting consisted of millions of determined people like Bloody Mary." Although Ratard was not pleased that Michener talked with Mary, the Frenchman had proof of Jim's "respect for French positions and . . . willingness to help him procure from the Navy tools and other necessities he needed for his plantation." Moreover, Ratard said that Mary was "one of the ablest of his work force."

Their forced indenture on Espíritu Santo prompted the Tonks to find additional ways to make money. Bloody Mary became something of a pest to American commanders by hawking her grass skirts and cheap necklaces to GIs from a little kiosk near the base. "Three dollars?" one GI suggested for a skirt. "Fo' dolla'!" cooed Mary. "'At's too much for a grass skirt, baby," he shot back. Mary would throw up her hands, scream an obscenity, and the serious bargaining would begin.

These two unlikely heroes—one a feisty Tonkinese survivor and the other a determined French planter—formed the nucleus of Michener's friendships on Santo. Although the beginnings of his first novel were some days and months away, Mary and Ratard were the early inspirations for his band of characters marooned by the war in the South Pacific.

•

Lieutenant Michener routinely made the 600-mile flight to the Solomons, northwest of the New Hebrides. It was probably the closest island chain to Santo that still remained tense and volatile. These missions involved carrying dispatches or inspecting the ground installations of Henderson Field on Guadalcanal.

The Solomons were composed of the larger islands of Bougainville and Choiseul to the northwest and New Georgia, Santa Isabel, Malaita, San Cristóbal, and Guadalcanal to the south. Smaller islands including Florida, Vella Lavella, Tulagi, and Savo also poked through the sea. Running directly from Bougainville to Guadalcanal with islands on either side was a broad avenue of contested water known as The Slot. In late 1942, American and Japanese naval forces fought viciously in this waterway, and Guadalcanal was retaken. By mid to late 1944 the Solomons, except for Bougainville, were in American hands.

On these junkets to Guadalcanal, Michener would stay in transient billets derisively labeled the Hotel de Gink. The original Hotel de Gink was erected in Seattle in 1913 and served as lodging for homeless people. "Gink" was a slang term for a bum or hobo. As military bases sprang up around the Pacific, ramshackle barracks were christened Hotels de Gink. They were popular in Samoa and Tonga as well as on Guadalcanal, which had the most famous one.

Sometimes hanging around for two or three days, Jim met various colorful characters in transit from the four corners of Pacific. Battle-weary pilots, Marine Corps sergeants, and navy commanders would huddle over their lukewarm beer in the breathless shade of banyan trees and share their

Jungle fighters on Bougainville, 1942. Many of these men were stationed on Espíritu Santo before being shipped out to attack strategic islands. Courtesy National Archives.

stories—the more outlandish the better. There was the navy flier who had to bail out into the waters of The Slot and who, after an intensive search, was finally rescued—at a cost of more than a half million dollars to the taxpayer. There was the resourceful sailor who, using old oil drums and rubber hoses, built a shower out from a tree. There was the raffish officer who refused to follow orders to blast an island monument which would allow for an American airstrip. There was the admiral who got his underwear caught in his zipper after using a latrine on Efate. "Goddamned things. I never wanted to buy them anyway," he roared. "Sold me a bill of goods." A chief machinist was enlisted to fix the zipper, but he was so drunk he ended up ripping the underwear. After some uncontrolled swearing, the admiral tossed the pants, underwear, and offending zipper in the trash.

But the story that riveted Michener involved the British, New Zealand, Australian, French, and Solomon Island coastwatchers who were scattered all over the island chain. Coastwatchers were crucial to naval commanders because they relayed enemy ship and troop movements to headquarters. Some were officials, while others were civilians. At the continual risk of their own lives, they broadcast reports and monitored the coastlines. In the oft-quoted opinion of Admiral William F. "Bull" Halsey, "the coast-watchers saved Guadalcanal and Guadalcanal saved the Pacific."

The coastwatchers transmitted their reports by teleradio, which could broadcast more than 400 miles by voice and 600 miles by Morse key, well beyond the limits of the Solomons. The Allies continuously monitored the network's emergency X frequency. Enemy movements on any given island in the Solomons or New Guinea could be flashed across the entire Pacific within minutes.

A second mission of the coastwatchers was rescuing civilians on threatened islands. Some island residents were reluctant to leave, as was the case with four American nuns on Bougainville just prior to the Japanese invasion. Coastwatcher Jack Read broadcast an urgent message directly to Admiral Halsey advising of their immediate danger should they stay and continue their missionary work. The nuns and twenty-five other civilians were ultimately rescued by an American submarine off Teop Harbor, Bougainville.

Other rescues involved downed American pilots and naval crews stranded by Japanese attacks on their ships. The most prominent beneficiary was future president John F. Kennedy. On August 2, 1943, in Blackett Strait of the Solomons, Lieutenant Kennedy was rescued by a coastwatcher after the PT (patrol torpedo) boat he commanded was rammed by a Japanese destroyer.

In the aftermath of the collision, Lieutenant Kennedy demonstrated conspicuous heroism. It was a dark night without a shaving of moon to light the murky waters. The impact of the destroyer knocked most of the crew of PT-109 overboard. While Kennedy swam around trying to assess the damage to his craft, many of his crew were sickened by fumes from spilled fuel. The PT boat was taking on water and in danger of exploding at any minute. Two of the crew had disappeared in the collision; the rest, with Kennedy guiding them, had to swim to land. In the darkness, however, they could make out nothing.

Kennedy had been on the swim team at Harvard; that experience served him well now, as he began heading away from his craft. One of his crew was badly injured, and so Kennedy towed him through the water by a belt clenched in his teeth. Two of the men, who could not swim at all, were lashed to a plank and pulled through the sea by other members of the crew. The nearest land was three and a half miles away. Hours later, after extreme physical exertion, the men arrived on a guano-covered islet called Plum Pudding, where they were eventually aided by an Australian coastwatcher and two natives. After the rescue Kennedy dismissed his bravery by laconically claiming: "It was involuntary. They sank my boat."

Martin Clemens, a Scot, was one of those brave and highly dependable coastwatchers. As a member of the British Colonial Service, Clemens was posted to the Solomons in the late 1930s. With the coming of the war, he volunteered to serve as a coastwatcher for the British Solomon Island Protectorate Defence Force. As the Japanese thrust toward the Solomons, Clemens went to work setting up his radio station and monitoring the

Captain Martin Clemens on Guadalcanal, 1942. Clemens, a British coastwatcher, was the inspiration for Michener's Remittance Man in *Tales of the South Pacific*. Courtesy National Archives.

coastline for enemy ships. When the battle for Guadalcanal intensified, Clemens headed up into a cave in the mountains, maintaining his daily broadcast to the American forces. With his supplies running low and his shoes disintegrating in the sodden jungle, he played daily cat-and-mouse with the Japanese.

Often at great risk to themselves, the coastwatchers sustained a punctual regimen of reporting. They also moved frequently, burrowing into their next hillside lair. Clemens became the inspiration for Michener's coastwatcher in *Tales of the South Pacific*, a Briton named Anderson known to the American troops as the Remittance Man. Always under the threat of Japanese reprisal, Anderson gave his daily broadcast from a secret location somewhere in the Solomons—probably on Bougainville—usually prefaced by weather conditions on the various islands around The Slot. After a detailed report on Japanese shipping, he ended his account with his signature lines: "Cheerio, Americans. Good hunting, lads."

When the conflict subsided in the Solomons, Clemens returned to his prewar activities. Michener's Remittance Man was not so fortunate. One day, as nervous listeners crowded around their radios, his broadcast was cut short by a gunshot. The Remittance Man had been discovered by the Japanese.

From New Guinea to the Solomons, from Guam to New Caledonia, the coastwatchers played a decisive role fighting Japanese aggression in the South Pacific. Michener was greatly impressed by their deeds and considered them as valorous as any man in uniform. And he honored them with a central role in his novel.

Nesomaniac

In 1890, after nearly two years of meandering through the islands of the South Pacific, the tubercular and celebrated Scottish author Robert Louis Stevenson settled down on four hundred lush mountain acres near Apia, Samoa. Along with his American wife Fanny, his stepson Lloyd, and his stepdaughter Belle, he erected a magnificent house on a hillside and christened it Vailima, meaning Five Rivers. He added a huge vegetable garden by clearing land, felling trees and hacking away at undergrowth that seemed to grow back overnight. As they settled into their new home, the Stevensons lived in constant fear of Louis's precarious health. Once in 1884 in Nice, Louis had experienced a serious infection of the kidneys and lungs. He hemorrhaged badly, sending geysers of blood everywhere. Before the doctor arrived, Fanny not only had to attend to a helpless man but also had to cope with the mental strain of trying to administer the proper first aid. In Samoa, realizing that the doctor was more than an hour away by horseback down the slopes in Apia, she became even more concerned that Louis would relapse.

For four years, however, Louis enjoyed relative good health. His writing blossomed once again and he produced some of his best work. *The Wrecker* and *The Ebb-Tide* were two of the novels he completed on the veranda or in the great room at Vailima. Waking at the Samoan dawn, watching the sun creep over dark green hills, he felt as energized as any time in his life. By embracing Samoa and its people, he had renounced civilization. "I was never fond of towns, society, or it seems civilization," he confessed in a letter to Henry James. "The sea islanders, the island life and climate, make me truly happier."

The Samoans, in return, loved Louis, calling him Tusitala, or Teller of Tales. They were, however, confused by the lavish lifestyle of Stevenson and his family at Vailima. To the Samoans, storytelling was not labor, so Louis really had no way of supporting such an estate. They concluded that Stevenson was a man of much *mana*, mysterious power, which the Polynesians believed came straight from heaven to the most powerful chiefs.

Stevenson's unabashed embrace of the South Pacific troubled his literary friends back home in Great Britain. They thought that Stevenson was squandering his literary career by living and cavorting with uncivilized and tattooed savages at the far end of the world. They sent him letters begging him to come home and write the works he was capable of writing. He did not heed them. Listening to the patient washing and moaning of the sea, he feverishly worked his pen and savored four years of relatively untroubled island bliss.

•

Fifty years after Stevenson's unexpected death from a brain hemorrhage in 1894, James Michener flew in to the airstrip near Apia on an unusual assignment: he was to investigate why an American general was building a road, at taxpayers' expense, the whole length of Samoa's most populous island. Michener was certainly as perplexed as his superiors. The only way to find an answer was to fly to the island, called Upolu, and talk to the people involved.

Before beginning his investigation, however, he climbed into a jeep and had his Samoan driver, Samosila, whisk him up the sinuous road to Stevenson's shrine overlooking the island's turquoise northern coast. An old caretaker appeared and showed Jim around the property. The garden was overgrown and in want of care. Presently Jim trudged up the hill and found Stevenson's grave bearing his famous epitaph: "Here he lies where he longed to be, / Home is the sailor, home from the sea, / And the hunter home from the hill."

Michener like Stevenson was an islomane, or, as he called himself, a nesomaniac—a person addicted to islands. Michener coined the term ("neso" in Greek means island) as early as 1931 while spending a few months in the Outer Hebrides off the coast of Scotland. "I was attuned to islands," he wrote. "I knew at first hand what life was like on the lonely atolls and the storm-swept islands that Joseph Conrad, Pierre Loti, Somerset Maugham, Alec Waugh, Jack London and Robert Louis Stevenson had loved. At times, working in big cities far from nature, I have been sick with nesomania, and I think the reason is this: On the islands one has both the time and the inclination to communicate with the stars and the trees and the waves drifting ashore, one lives more intensely."

As prolific islomanes, these writers and nomads of Oceania had nothing over Michener. He visited nearly fifty islands during his navy duty. Some were brief encounters; others, perhaps twenty in number, were intimate and enduring associations with some of the major islands of the South Pacific. Michener wondered why he seemed condemned to travel so much. Was it "some psychic maladjustment," a "sickness of spirit," or "the mere perversity of a restless young male" with which he had been afflicted? At various times in his life, the question had been raised and then as quickly dropped again.

He returned to the house and walked up some rickety steps to the library. Many of the volumes Stevenson had had shipped from Scotland, but a few had accompanied him on his South Pacific odyssey. Herman Melville, the literary culprit most responsible for sending so many Europeans to the South Seas, had a treasured place on Stevenson's shelf. Jim found copies of *Typee* and *Omoo*, the classic, risqué, and often embellished accounts of Melville's sojourn in French Polynesia in 1842–43. They were Stevenson's *Iliad* and *Odyssey*, if not his bibles while in the South Pacific. A photograph of Melville stood upright in a frame next to *Typee*.

Since Melville feared the intimacy of the camera, there are very few photographs of him. Those few reveal a man sharply at odds with his world. The hair is thick and majestic. The crinkly beard cascades like Moses'. The mouth is firm and resolute. But the eyes—ah, the eyes—gaze beyond the viewer to a distant horizon, as if Melville's landlocked existence among the respectable people of New England was a slow, silent torture.

From the very beginning Melville loved the sea. In 1841, at the age of twenty-two, he was aboard the whaling ship *Acushnet* bound for the South Pacific via Cape Horn. One of his destinations was Nuku Hiva in the Marquesas, part of French Polynesia, an island group attractive enough to lure the peripatetic Michener on his first tour of duty in the South Pacific.

As D. H. Lawrence has suggested, the Pacific Ocean is richer historically and culturally than the Atlantic. It is also far older: "The Maoris, the Marquesans, the Fijians, the Polynesians: holy God, how long have they been turning over in the same sleep, with varying dreams? . . . The heart of the Pacific is still the Stone Age, in spite of steamers. The heart of the Pacific seems like a vast vacuum, in which, mirage-like, continues the life of ages back."

Into this veritable Stone Age world Melville sailed. After six months at sea, the *Acushnet* arrived in the harbor of Nuku Hiva. Melville looked at paradise for the first time. With the arms of the bay flung wide, the wet vegetation heaving and swelling in the southeasterly breeze, and the chattering of wildlife, the island throbbed with physical and sexual energy.

On the voyage he had made friends with a shipmate named Toby, a footloose soldier of fortune. Toby was close to Melville's size, just under five foot ten, with somber eyes and a dense matting of hair that could have doubled as a robin's nest. Together they hatched a plot to desert the ship and live off the fruits of the island. Toby (his real name was Richard Tobias Greene) became Melville's companion for at least part of their sojourn on Nuku Hiva. One night they slipped over the side of the *Acushnet*, swam to shore, and disappeared into the dense thickets bordering the beach. Thus began the adventure that became the greatest of all South Sea romantic narratives, and the one that both Stevenson and Michener mined repeatedly in their fiction.

A few years later in 1846, a remarkable first novel appeared on London bookstalls. The following month Wiley and Putnam brought out the American edition titled *Typee: A Peep at Polynesian Life*, detailing Melville's three-week stay on Nuku Hiva. In the narrative, however, his speedy visit is lengthened to four months. The author was not an ethnologist, historian, or sociologist, but a mere whaler deckhand who related a romantic adventure among the fierce Typee natives of the Marquesas Islands.

Suspicious editors, quick to realize the story was too good to be true, dubbed it a work of fiction, albeit convincing and adventurous fiction. Fearing a backlash of indignant readers, Wiley's editors had scrupulously gone over Melville's manuscript and penciled out numerous passages too spicy for a high-minded American audience. For instance, publisher Joseph Wiley had deleted the scene of a native princess who "threw up her skirts" to reveal tattooed buttocks. Other references to the incident inciting "the unholy passions of the crew" were similarly excised. Melville's book, although popular in the public imagination, was not a huge success, selling six thousand copies in the first two years. But it was a book that seemed to be on everyone's lips.

For one thing, it was a fascinating tale. During his sojourn with the Typee natives, Melville encountered cannibalism and the ritual practice of tattooing. He discovered that the Marquesan natives had raised tattooing to the highest levels of art, creating some of the most sophisticated and intricate designs in the South Pacific. Among certain warriors, the whole body could be covered in ink, including face, eyelids, hands, and buttocks. Despite his deep fears, Melville was tempted to get his own tattoo, particularly when the Typee king demanded that Melville demonstrate his courage. However, he could not bring himself to cross that barrier. Fearing that his "face divine" would become "hideous for life" and render him a freak among his friends back home, he rejected the idea.

The lovely and entrancing Fayaway was another story. She had three little tattooed dots on her upper and lower lip that accentuated her loveliness. With magnificent hair falling in waves, and clothed only in the "summer garb of Eden," she exhausted all descriptions and adjectives. In Melville's novel, she was the prototype of all Polynesian women romanced by European males. Melville's brief but passionate interlude with Fayaway influenced several generations of similar romances, from Gauguin and Stevenson to Conrad, James Norman Hall, James A. Michener, and the fighting men of the Second World War. In many cases, the relationships ended in tragedy.

Who could forget the scene in *Typee* when the narrator accompanies the beautiful Fayaway on a canoe trip in the verdant valley? As Melville stares breathlessly up at her, she rises and unties her tapa, allowing the breeze to fill it like a sail. Carried along by the wind, her nude body stretched out like a mast, her long tresses streaming in the air, the canoe glides effortlessly. In this idyllic valley, Fayaway caters to his every need and fulfills his every desire. Very much a young woman, and at the same time a fantasy figure for Melville, she is exciting without being lewd, alluring without being wanton.

After his sojourn on the island reached its apogee, and convinced that the "savages" regarded him more as a captive than a tourist, Melville made his escape in an Australian whaleboat. Arriving back in America in October of 1844, he quickly set about launching a literary career by recording his own experiences in *Typee* and *Omoo*, the original tales of the South Pacific.

Melville, Stevenson, and later James Michener stood in a long line of notable literary, and mostly male, nesomaniacs (although Lawrence Durrell's later term "islomane" seems to have become more popular). Islands have a way of inspiring, of soothing rattled nerves, of creating or destroying personalities. Islands have revealed guilt and expiation in Defoe's *Robinson Crusoe*, adolescent evil in Golding's *Lord of the Flies*, greed and treachery in Stevenson's *Treasure Island*, supernatural intrigue in Verne's *Mysterious Island*, and belated moral awareness in Conrad's *Victory*. One of the more trenchant and unsettling accounts of islomanes is D. H. Lawrence's short story "The Man Who Loved Islands," a contemporary fable of attraction gone awry. Lawrence, who always liked and feared being alone, once observed: "Isolate yourself on an island, in a sea of space, and the moment begins to heave . . . the solid earth is gone, and your slippery naked dark soul finds herself out in the timeless world. . . . The souls of the dead are alive again, and pulsating actively around you. You are out in the other infinity." In Lawrence's story a man named Cathcart, sick of modern mechanization and technology, forsakes his comfortable world and buys an island off the English coast, hoping to make it his own small utopia. Eventually his enterprise loses money, a gale wrecks his boat, and the few inhabitants of the island begin to battle each other. His second island, hardly more than a speck of rock, he shares with five of his most trusted friends. After a bitter affair with the daughter of his housekeeper, he flees to a third island, which is even smaller and more remote. On this third island, a few acres of wind-raked barren soil, he builds a stone house and briefly enjoys his castaway existence. At last finding a place where "time had ceased to pass," he eventually succumbs to delirium and loses his grip on reality.

As refuge or crucible or cemetery, islands' fascination for writers seems never ending.

·

Just before sunset, Samosila drove Jim down the mountain to Apia, where he would stay for the duration of his visit. As the day melted into night and the road curved along the beach, they saw men and women stream from the villages and head down to the water. Wading in, they threw of their sarongs and frolicked aimlessly in the ocean before retiring for the night.

There was no debate about where Jim would stay while in Apia. Samosila drove directly to the Cosmopolitan Club in the heart of the city.

Run by Aggie Grey, the daughter of a Scottish adventurer and a Samoan woman, the rambling white hotel and bar started out modestly in the 1930s. Guests sat on the floor and drank beer and whisky. Americans poured in from the U.S. naval base on Pago Pago eighty miles away, which was under a strict prohibition order. Soon Aggie's place got the reputation of being the mecca of Samoa. She started selling hamburgers to hungry GIs. Tom Collins became the favorite cocktail. "Boy that Tom Collins," exclaimed Aggie. "The Americans drank so much of it I was shoving dollars under the mat, under the icebox and everywhere."

By 1941 she was making enough money to begin upgrading the facilities. She added a real bar and expanded the number of hotel rooms. For Michener such a watering hole became irresistible. Guzzling a cold beer on a hot island night was something of a luxury. In addition, Samoan music serenaded the throngs, and a bevy of island women wandered among the American and European patrons.

Like the Hotel de Gink on Guadalcanal, the Cosmopolitan Club produced some the best tales of the war. "I think half of the good stories I heard about the war reached me at Aggie Grey's," said Michener. Aggie also joined in the action on the dance floor. Tall and lithe with a pronounced alto voice, she enjoyed doing the uniquely Samoan dance called the siva-siva, which involved a great deal of skill and hip-swaying. "No one did the siva better than Aggie," remarked Jim, "and as the evenings wore on she would called upon many times to join some admiral or general as he tried in his inept way to copy her movements."

The bond between Michener and Aggie Grey lasted a lifetime, and he frequently commented on their special relationship. He even mentioned that she in some way modeled some of the traits of Bloody Mary in *Tales of the South Pacific*. From these comments came the perception from some observers that she was Bloody Mary. This is not the case. The one and only Bloody Mary was Tonkinese and she lived as an indentured servant on Espíritu Santo. Over the years, Aggie developed her hotel in Apia, and Jim never missed an opportunity to stop in and visit her.

However, Aggie did figure prominently in Michener's first assignment in British Samoa. After interviewing some people in Apia, Jim learned more of the American general who had built a road from the north coast of this island to the south coast. He had built the road, the story went, because he wanted comfortable access to the house of his newfound love—a young, beautiful Samoan woman who turned out to be Aggie

Grey's sister. The general, who had transferred the cost of the road to the American taxpayer, had left for frontline duty farther north.

Not wishing to jeopardize his relationship with Aggie over this delicate matter, Michener ultimately decided to file his report using the most nonjudgmental terms possible. After driving the entire route from coast to coast and weighing the human costs of his investigation, he added a final note: "If the Japanese *had* invaded the north side of Upolu and *had* tried to attack the south side, this road would have been quite valuable to the American defenses."

Michener filed his report; it was accepted by his superiors, and no further questions were asked.

•

Back on Santo, he received his new assignment, which took him from a stack of reports and sent him to the neighboring island of Aoba. The navy wished formally to recognize the services to American fliers that villages in the Solomons performed during the early days of the war. One of those villages, a school administered by a woman known as Mother Margaret, had been on Tulagi before the Japanese swept through in 1942. Mother Margaret had fled six hundred miles southeast to Aoba with some of her students and had tried to revitalize her school on that island. Michener, accompanied by a local guide, carried with him the promise of clothing, food, and supplies to assist Mother Margaret in her venture.

"We coasted along the forbidding island for two days," wrote Michener. "At night we lay off the fever-ridden shore and listened to the soft jungle sounds. Early on the third day we went ashore. . . . We walked through dense jungle for about an hour and came finally upon a clearing. An astonishing sight greeted us." They were surrounded by seventy dark Melanesian girls, laughing and following them to several rows of bamboo huts. Gardens filled with corn, yams, watermelon, and taro surrounded the huts. A gray-haired white woman, perhaps fifty years old, approached them.

"She was as stately as a queen," noted Jim. "Nobility spoke in every movement she made. She was barefoot. Her feet were splayed and hard. She wore a kind of sacking for a dress. Her hands were rough from heavy work and her handsome face was weather-beaten."

She introduced herself as Mother Margaret. Michener told her about his mission to find the brave men responsible for rescuing American pilots and reward them with gifts. Margaret pointed to one of the young girls. "There's your man." She laughed. "Yes, that girl saved the Americans. When their planes went down offshore, she paddled out and dragged them into her canoe."

After rewarding the girl, he turned to Mother Margaret, hoping to learn more of her struggles and challenges. Mother Margaret, then called Sister Margaret Pears Wilson, had arrived in the Solomons from Great Britain in the early 1930s and helped develop the Anglican missionary system. By 1936 she helped found several girls' schools on the islands of Bungana and Malaita and the principal one, called the School Island, on Tulagi. Melanesian girls from all over the Solomon Islands attended the school. Mother Margaret and several Sisters of the Cross instructed the young girls in agriculture, weaving, fishing, and eradicating mosquitoes. One of her fellow missionaries, Sister Veronica of the Cross, kept a journal of those seminal years which she published in 1949 under the title *The School Island*. Among other things, it recorded Mother Margaret's accomplishments amid the squalid conditions of the Solomons and her eventual departure:

> On 1 December 1941 the School Island said good-bye to Mother Margaret who, with two of the Melanesian Sisters, was going to look after the school in the New Hebrides. Less than a week later the war with Japan started. The School Island was only a quarter of a square mile, but it was so placed in Tulagi Harbour as to be of strategic importance.
> . . . [In January] Japanese reconnaissance planes sometimes came over flying very high, but it was not until noon of 22 January that the bombing of Tulagi began. Sister Gwen and Sister Madeleine had been shopping that morning; they bought the last pair of shoes ever purchased in Tulagi, and had an extra pair pressed upon them as a gift. Ten minutes after they arrived back at Taroaniara the first bomber came over. The School, in their khaki skirts, faded into the bush near by. No one can do that more silently and speedily than a Melanesian.

Mother Margaret and her mission school on Aoba reignited Michener's fervent ideas about education. "Here was teaching I had never known before," he wrote. "Here was the very essence of all that education stands for: a dedicated human being tearing the lessons from the world's past experience and sharing it with . . . children." Noting the school's lack of adequate books, he told Mother Margaret, "As soon as possible, I'm going to cable for a complete library. You'll have so many beautiful books . . . well, you won't have room for them all!"

After returning to duty, Michener dashed off a note to his boss at Macmillan, the president and CEO George P. Brett Jr., in which he related how he had met this wonderful, dedicated teacher in the New Hebrides in need of a library of books. Shortly thereafter, Michener received a copy of Brett's letter to Mother Margaret:

> This morning I have received a letter from your friend and mine, Lieut. James A. Michener, in which he has told me of the magnificent work that you are doing in the New Hebrides and in which he has suggested that you really should have some of our books at your disposal. Indeed, the Lieutenant has suggested that I send you these books and charge his account. Well, they are coming from him with his compliments, but the Macmillan Company is not going to allow him to pay for them. Perhaps then I may be forgiven for taking the ball and running with it.

> I am enclosing a list of the books we are shipping so that you may see what is on the way to you. It may take some time to get these books under way as we are limited as to the amount of books we may ship to the New Hebrides, but I am endeavoring to get government assistance to ship all of these at one time, and you will get them eventually.

Brett further mentioned that he was envious of his "young friend" the lieutenant, and expressed the hope that, after the war, "it will be possible for me to take a trip which will fulfill my desire to learn more of the world and the people in it, how they live, and what can be done to help them, such as the things you are doing."

Two Tales

Admiral Halsey's fleet headquarters in Nouméa on the French island of New Caledonia witnessed a steady stream of senior naval officers, and none seemed to be a more frequent presence than Vice Admiral William "Billy" Calhoun, the man most responsible for the unimpeded flow of men and materiel from America to the South Pacific. Halsey's and Calhoun's personalities were in brilliant counterpoint. Halsey was gruff, loquacious, and implacable; Calhoun, a grandson of the famous senator John C. Calhoun, was calm, direct, and affable. A firm teetotaler, he took a brisk walk every day and before church on Sunday. Halsey liked to smoke, and to eat lunch shirtless under a palm tree, displaying an anchor tattoo on his right arm, a bit of pictorial whimsy that he claimed signified his "sea-dogginess."

Six months into his stint in the tropics, Lieutenant James A. Michener had achieved a stellar reputation as an ombudsman for the U.S. Navy. If there was some problem on a far-flung island involving American interests, Michener was the man to resolve it. He had recently been promoted to full lieutenant.

Thus there seemed nothing out of the ordinary when Michener was summoned to headquarters in Nouméa. He took the first military hop from Santo, a veteran DC-3, and flew in to the Tontouta airstrip serving the New Caledonian capital. Standing before Admiral Calhoun, he heard: "They tell me, Michener, that you know the islands. I want you to take a swing and find out what's happening on Bora Bora. We're having a lot of trouble with the enlisted men."

Michener ventured that the enlisted men were chafing to get home.

"No," Calhoun said. "Trouble with this crowd is, they don't want to go home, and when we try to send them, they raise merry hell."

"Never heard of such a thing."

"Nor anybody. Now get out there and find out."

Before Michener withdrew, an aide came in and gave him some additional assignments, including one for the final leg of his swing through French Polynesia.

"On the remote atoll of Pukapuka, far from Tahiti," said the aide, "there's a beachcombing American writer, broken-down chap, married an island girl and all that—three kids, maybe five or six. Natives have reported by radio he's been using the needle and is dying. Fly up there and see what's to be done."

"What's his name? Maybe I know him."

"Robert Dean Frisbie. Those who know him tell us his books are first class, but nobody's seen any of them. Anyway, we can't leave an American citizen dying on some atoll. Hurricane could sweep him away."

Toting his briefcase, Michener hurried out by jeep to the Tontouta airstrip to begin his assignment. He soon hooked up with "a tough crew of four who had flown their miracle DC-3 to all parts of the southeastern war zone: New Caledonia to Tahiti. . . . I had little confidence in some of the other planes I had flown in, especially the tricky B-26s, which tended to go down on takeoff if improperly balanced, but the DC-3s I could depend on to fly me anywhere and get me safely back."

The thousand-mile, seven-hour flight to Bora Bora gave Jim adequate time to review his assignment and contemplate the island's singular reputation. The jewel of French Polynesia, it was widely considered the most beautiful island in the South Pacific, if not the world. Set in the satiny waters, its dark volcanic neck rose starkly from the varying shades of green jungle surrounding it. From the air it presented a magical, fairy-tale quality, far from the strife of war and seemingly in its own universe.

That it was even on the American military's map owed something to a roll of the dice. The navy needed a strategic fueling station that would keep the sea lanes open from French Polynesia to Australia. In February 1942 the first detachment of Seabees landed on Bora Bora and immediately turned it into a serviceable military island.

Despite diseases ranging from elephantiasis to dysentery, the island quickly became a Melvillean paradise for the troops. They rarely saw action. They had girlfriends from the local population. They watched Hollywood movies. In short, life was as good here as anyplace in the States. Why wouldn't any sailor protest leaving the island?

The situation on Bora Bora intrigued Michener. Everything about the island appeared unique: the perfect lime-green coral reef ten miles in diameter surrounding the island, the great pillar of rock rising from an ancient volcano, the airstrip built of shimmering white coral on which his DC-3 bounced along and finally came to a stop.

After meeting with French government officials and an American naval lieutenant, Michener put together the facts of the issue: A twenty-year-old navy seaman from Alabama by the name of Gosford had arrived on Bora Bora in mid-1942. He had performed his duties in an exemplary fashion and he seemed to adapt immediately to the relaxed lifestyle on the island. He met and fell in love with a Polynesian woman named Terua. Now she was pregnant with his child. He agreed that it was his time to rotate back to America or to another duty station nearer the fighting. However, he wanted to wait several months until his baby was born.

When his mother got word that his tour of duty on Bora Bora was exceeding the normal limit, she became alarmed. She sought the help of her congressman, who intervened and urged the Navy Department to ship Seaman Gosford home. When Halsey and Calhoun heard that a congressman had gotten involved, it was time to put pressure on the military on Bora Bora.

During a slow, deliberate interview with Gosford, Michener probed the sailor's commitment to his island duty. "You don't want to go home?" asked Michener.

"Nobody on this rock wants to go home."

"What's happening, then?"

"I may have to go. . . . It's Mom. She insists I come home. . . . She hears about other men from the war front, they come home after eighteen months."

The whole issue was becoming quite contentious: an anxious mother back in Alabama, an insistent congressman, a pregnant young woman, and a reluctant seaman. Michener suggested that once his mother knew about the impending birth, she and the congressman might relent and let him stay through Terua's pregnancy. Michener could arrange for the navy, then, to grant "compassionate understanding."

Gosford recoiled. "Oh, Lieutenant Michener! No! No! It would kill my mother. . . . She would have to find out sooner or later that Terua was a nigger."

Michener said he could keep the whole issue secret. But Seaman Gosford insisted that eventually the truth would emerge that he and Terua were "having a nigger baby."

Michener's lengthy report foreshadowed the scope of some of his later novels. In the end, the home front won out: Seaman Gosford was ordered back to America on the next plane. But the Gosford affair went beyond the mere removal of a forlorn seaman. Michener viewed the incident as one of the most memorable of the war, largely because it touched upon issues of racial ignorance, hatred, and injustice. The Gosford-Terua affair would inspire the events in *Tales of the South Pacific* in which love affairs are tortured and broken by racial intolerance.

As he traveled throughout the South Pacific, Michener was troubled by the American attitudes toward other races, attitudes exacerbated by the war. The Japanese soldier in particular was singled out for vilification. The attack on Pearl Harbor and the early successes of Japan's navy, combined with America's longstanding prejudice against Asians in general, produced deep-seated hatred of Japanese men in uniform. Many Americans considered them to be "ungodly, subhuman, beastly, sneaky, and treacherous." While German soldiers in films were routinely portrayed as efficient and disciplined, Japanese were often depicted as ruthless and cruel. The Japanese soldiers were "small, wiry, and wore spectacles. They were tough but devoid of scruples. They flashed repulsive buck-tooth grins and reveled in bayoneting helpless prisoners of war."

Japan had not ratified the Geneva Convention that called for the humane treatment of prisoners of war and noncombatants. With the treatment of POWs and captured civilians left to the discretion of the unit commanders, the Japanese relied on their Bushido code, a fierce warrior mentality that demanded that no soldier surrender or otherwise weaken his samurai masculinity. Virtually no Japanese army detachment surrendered during the war, so that the Allies had to torch whole islands in order to occupy them. Loathing of the Japanese ran up the chain of command. Admiral Halsey had a particularly strong antipathy. He ordered that the rock entrances to Tulagi harbor in the Solomons be painted with the huge letters KILL, KILL, KILL, KILL MORE JAPS—HALSEY, so that advancing American forces could see their mission plain and simple.

In America this hatred was an enormously powerful force. In 1942 President Roosevelt authorized the internment not only of Japanese resident aliens but of citizens of Japanese descent. More than one hundred thousand people were removed from California to camps in Nevada, Utah, and Colorado, including a twenty-two-year-old Japanese-American woman named Mari Sabusawa, James Michener's future wife, who with her family was interned at a desolate camp in eastern Colorado. All were forced to leave their homes and to liquidate their savings.

Asians and Pacific Islanders tended to be lumped together. Polynesians, Melanesians, Micronesians, Maoris, and Indonesians were viewed as one people, even though they had vastly different cultures. A host of romantic tales fed the popular perception of Polynesian women as possessive, al-luring, and sexually immoral—hence the treatment of the relationship of Seaman Gosford and Terua. As Michener journeyed throughout the Pacific, these stereotypes became even more evident.

But the setting outshone this particular incident. Upon leaving, Jim reflected on his sojourn and called Bora Bora, most emphatically, "the most beautiful island in the world."

.

Like Robert Louis Stevenson and so many others, Robert Dean Frisbie fled to the South Pacific because of failing health. Born in Cleveland in 1896, he served in World War I and in 1920 went into self-imposed exile in Tahiti. He became a plantation owner and travel writer, sending back to America a plethora of travel articles relating to Polynesia. He also be-came an islomane's islomane. In Tahiti he met the writing team of Charles Nordhoff and James Norman Hall, later famous for the trilogy of books beginning in 1932 with *Mutiny on the Bounty*.

Nordhoff and Hall were writers similarly impacted by health concerns and the horrors of World War I. Seeking sanctuary away from civilization and its seemingly endless cycles of war, they landed in Tahiti in the same year as Frisbie, although they did not meet until some months later. Hall, born in Iowa, became the spokesperson for the writing team and its major contributor. The pair encouraged Frisbie in his writing before he moved to the lonely atoll of Pukapuka in the Cook Islands. In 1928 he married a sixteen-year-old island woman, with whom he had five children. Over the next few years Frisbie continued an extensive interpretation of Poly-nesian life, writing in the process his first and most acclaimed work, *The Book of Puka-Puka* (1929). Back in America he was read widely, although his novels did not have the impact of his fellow islomanes Nordhoff and Hall's *Bounty* trilogy; the first book in that trio, *Mutiny on the Bounty*, was filmed in 1935 and several times thereafter.

As the 1930s advanced and war loomed, Frisbie's wife died. Now living on Penrhyn Atoll northwest of Pukapuka in the Cook Islands, he continued to raise his children and write his articles and novels. In his mid-forties, with his tuberculosis worsening, he was a frail wizened man with a lantern jaw. Continuing his love-hate relationship with atolls—in which the love always seemed to win out—he was finally brought low by his disease in 1943. The word went out to the U.S. Navy that Frisbie needed an emergency airlift to the nearest American hospital, which happened to be in American Samoa.

As Michener's plane approached Penrhyn Atoll, he reflected on Frisbie's contribution to his knowledge of Oceania. Because Michener was a scholar of literature and not yet a writer of any merit, he viewed Frisbie with a devotion that bordered on hero worship. "I had never met Frisbie," he wrote, "but I had read one of his books that had been recommended to me by an Australian who had given it the same high praise as Hall. It was a lovely, relaxed account of life in the area I was coming to know so well, and it was obvious to me, having once been a book editor, that if Frisbie got hold of himself he could write a fine novel about the kind of adventures he'd had." With some variations, the Frisbie story was well known throughout the American colony in Polynesia. People usually told Michener that Frisbie had great talent but was "self-destructive" and "doomed." Further, he was "a cantankerous son-of-a-bitch" who would not let anybody help him.

With these ideas in mind, Michener watched as his plane drifted toward the speck of land in the blue ocean that was Penrhyn Atoll. "It was a place of utter loneliness," Michener remarked, "the end of the world, and all who saw it for the first time in those years had the same thought: Come a major hurricane . . . this place is a goner." The plane dropped lower, and its wheels soon gripped the crude airstrip. After it came to a stop, the crew put down the ramp, and Jim descended. In front of him stood Frisbie, his soiled shirt flapping around his gaunt frame, his fine hair torn by the sea breeze, his feet encased in stained sneakers. Michener introduced himself and shook Frisbie's weak hand. Next to Frisbie stood four of his children, three girls and a boy, between the ages of ten and fourteen.

Michener knew he had to get Frisbie aboard quickly and off to Samoa, leaving the children on the atoll. After Frisbie was settled on the plane, Jim collected some money from the crew, ran back down the stairs, and stuffed the American dollar bills into the oldest daughter's hand. He embraced her and whispered: "We'll save your father and we'll come back to rescue you."

Ten minutes later they were lifting off the airstrip and banking toward American Samoa and the hospital. Michener looked back and saw the four children still standing next to the runway. During the flight, Jim periodically cradled Frisbie's head in his lap, while the author related the events of his past: how he came to the South Pacific, how he settled among the little atolls, how he met his island wife, how he eked out a living as a writer.

For Michener, such private moments with a writer of some stature proved both influential and inspirational. In the back of Jim's mind, the thought persisted: perhaps I too can find a voice to tell my version of the South Pacific war. Frisbie's courage, his humanity, his willingness to stay on his atoll to the bitter end, moved Jim deeply.

By the time they arrived in Samoa, Frisbie's condition had worsened. An ambulance met the plane. As the patient was transferred on a stretcher, Jim told Frisbie his children would be taken care of—a promise Jim made good on. The doctor in charge whisked Frisbie away in the ambulance, leaving Michener to hope Frisbie could be taken care of too.

Tontouta

The waning months of 1944 saw stunning and decisive victories for the Allies in the South Pacific. Successive battles in the Philippines and the Leyte Gulf brought the American navy and marines fresh hope that the war was winding to a close. As with most campaigns involving many branches of the military, some saw action while others, like Michener and many of the Seabees on Santo, remained idle. A sailor on the USS *Enterprise*, for example, would have been involved in most of the naval actions in the Pacific War. But for the vast majority of military personnel, the war was characterized by incessant waiting. Of the army and air force troops involved in the Pacific campaign, only a third saw battle. For Michener this disparity produced guilt, but he remained hopeful that he was contributing something of value. "I was always mindful," he remarked, "that while I was exploring the joyous wonders of Polynesia many of my friends were landing on quite different islands. Tarawa, Saipan, and Okinawa. I never forgot that difference."

Most of Jim's distant assignments required that he return to Admiral Halsey's headquarters in Nouméa and file his report before heading back to Espíritu Santo. Such was the case one late afternoon as his DC-3 approached the Tontouta airstrip. Located eighteen miles outside Nouméa on the only plausible terrain, the Tontouta airstrip was none too long and ended at an unforgiving range of mountains. Even in good weather, landing was a challenge. That day, however, a tropical thunderstorm was brewing, and it swallowed the plane on its final approach to Tontouta.

Witnessing a thunderstorm in the tropics inspires awe; landing in one provokes sheer panic. As rain pelted the windows and cut visibility to zero, and the descending plane slowed toward stall speed, Michener and the other passengers braced themselves. Suddenly the pilot pulled up and swerved back over the ocean. He made a second approach, as abortive as the first. With fuel running low, the pilot swung back over the sea for his third attempt. This time he set the plane down on the slick runway and brought it to a stop at the very end of the airstrip.

That night, unable to sleep, Michener left his transient quarters and walked along the runway reliving the frightening moments of that afternoon. "What do I want to do with the remainder of my life?" he asked himself. "What do I stand for? What do I hope to accomplish with the years that will be allowed me? Do I really want to go back to what I was doing before?" Pacing along the airstrip, he probed his deepest conscience. He had to admit to himself that, while his present life was a colorful one, flitting about the South Pacific like a young vagabond, he had no center. He had no deep convictions about his life and how it was to take shape. From that experience on the Tontouta airstrip, Jim ultimately decided: "I'm going to live the rest of my life as if I were a great man." To this end, he promised himself that he would "erase envy and cheap thoughts" and would tackle "objectives of the moment."

On returning to Santo, Jim began to formulate how to put these lofty ambitions into practice. First, he got serious about his writing. Not that there was an overwhelming need to put words on paper. "I didn't say, 'I'm going to be a writer,'" he recalled later. "All I knew was that I could write a lot better than the stuff I was reading. I was going to take a shot at it." The typewriter in his Quonset was an aching reminder of his idleness. His own experiences and the tales told to him suddenly cried out to him. "I'm going to write down as simply and honestly as I can what it was really like," he wrote. "No one knows the Pacific better than I do; no one can tell the story more accurately."

He was at first intimidated by the significant tradition of South Pacific literature. Next to Melville, Stevenson, Conrad, Maugham, or the more contemporary popular fictionists like Frederick O'Brien (*White Shadows in the South Seas*), James Norman Hall, and Robert Dean Frisbie, he felt a twinge of inadequacy. Added to this was his lack of preparation in fiction writing. He had only written some maudlin poetry in college, a few pieces for academic journals, and the truncated beginnings of several novels, filed away, never to be resurrected. Still, he would at least "give it a shot."

His newfound commitment to himself, consecrated on the runway at Tontouta, bolstered his sense of purpose.

Once he had mustered his courage, things moved swiftly. At nine-thirty each night he would return to his Quonset hut, light a lantern to keep away the mosquitoes, and sit at his bulky typewriter, slowly pecking out stories. "Sitting there in the darkness," Jim commented, "I visualized the aviation scenes in which I had participated, the landing beaches I'd seen, the remote outposts . . . and especially the valiant people I'd known." By his typewriter he kept photos of key people to help write descriptions of them.

His philosophy in writing his tales of the South Pacific remained simple: he would stay away from the heroics and romanticism of past writers and concentrate on the simple follies and deeds of the fighting men of the navy and army. He would also focus on the lives of various women, because they were as much a part of the South Pacific experience as the men at arms.

His selection of an appropriate narrator became the key to the book. The unnamed narrator was a person similar to Michener in some qualities but unlike him in others: a naval historian, well educated but not intellectual, curious but not imaginative, practical without being too boring. He was a middle-class Midwestern American naval lieutenant who could insinuate himself into any situation and record its proceedings. He was neither too literary nor too ignorant of convention. Michener also used the unusual device of having his narrator witness scenes and hear conversations that were miles away.

Of all the twentieth-century writers who wrote of the South Seas, Michener was particularly indebted to Somerset Maugham, who used the device of the detached narrator to great effect in the novels *The Moon and Sixpence, Cakes and Ale,* and *The Razor's Edge.* After some deliberation, Michener finally chose this narrative technique for his first work of fiction. The detached narrator is in the story, but not part of it. In *Tales* he functions as a kind of trustworthy everyman; the Tonkinese and the military open up to him. Generally, however, Michener's unnamed narrator is self-effacing and uninvolved. His role is to keep the story moving and to provide tonal continuity to the various episodes. While Maugham's narrator is often an urbane, sophisticated traveler given to clubbing along Pall Mall and haunting the National Gallery, Michener's prefers having a beer at the Officer's Club.

After the war, Michener noted in a letter to a friend: "One of the evil limitations put on anyone who wants to write about the South Pacific is that he must stop reading Maugham and Conrad, lest he inadvertently plagiarize from those masters." In the same letter, he acknowledged the influence of Maugham in beginning his novels: "Before I start to do any writing about this vast area I usually take down 'Rain' and reread those first three paragraphs to remind myself of how completely one can set a physical stage in a few absolutely correct observations. I hold those passages to be about the best beginning of a mood story extant." Set in Samoa during the second decade of the twentieth century, "Rain" features the disintegration of Sadie Thompson, a down-on-her-luck prostitute in Pago Pago. As Michener acknowledged in his letter, it became a perennial treasure trove.

Michener outlined eighteen chapters, and thus began a tradition of "seeing" the whole book from start to finish. In his mind he knew each plot turn and how each character contributed to the whole. He added the first chapter, titled "The South Pacific," to give the book its tone and atmosphere. "I wish I could tell you about the South Pacific . . . ," it begins. "But whenever I try to talk about the South Pacific, people intervene." The opening three pages—no more than two thousand words—are as seductive as the beginning of any novel to emerge from the Second World War. The narrator slips smoothly from his inability to describe the war to introducing a host of colorful characters who constantly tug at his sleeve for attention. Here Michener clearly demonstrates his debt to Maugham and the importance of establishing interest and mood from the first sentence. The remaining eighteen tales are independent of each other, except that certain characters in earlier stories reappear later. These connections serve as the loose threads that weave the tales together. All stories anticipate the major military operation known as Operation Alligator, which Michener probably based on Operation Galvanic to invade Tarawa in 1943.

His characters Tony Fry, Bus Adams, Ensign Bill Harbison, the Remittance Man, Luther Billis, Atabrine Benny, Lieutenant Joe Cable, and Ensign Nellie Forbush were based on real characters that Michener had met, or were composites. The French plantation owner on Santo, Aubert Ratard, became Emile de Becque; his Tonkinese laborer Bloody Mary retained her real name—the only character in the book to do so. Michener also added minor characters such as Admiral Kester, who was partly based on Admiral Billy Calhoun on New Caledonia.

As his early biographer John Hayes wrote, Jim created a multilayered work depicting "(1) navy life, with its boredom and comedy, its jealousies and antagonisms; (2) a romantic desire for beauty, love, tranquillity; (3) the granite facts of military struggle; and (4) the impact of two alien cultures on each other—of airplanes, jeeps, bulldozers, marines, and canned goods superimposed on a simple, natural life on the most peaceful, most beautiful islands in the world."

Michener dealt head-on with the subject of racial discrimination and prejudice. As early as the mid-1920s, when he was an undergraduate at Swarthmore, he loathed people who looked down on minorities, and he frequently campaigned against elite fraternities that discriminated against blacks and Jews. In 1936, while a professor at the University of Northern Colorado, he fought for migrant workers' rights in the sugar beet fields of Greeley. In his first book, he would not only probe the most blatant forms of prejudice between cultures but also expose its more sinister aspects within the United States military. The Gosford-Terua affair would be moved center stage and used as the basis for the fictional Lieutenant Cable to end his liaison with the no longer virginal Liat, Bloody Mary's daughter. Entrenched prejudice would also serve to drive a wedge between Ensign Nellie Forbush and Emile de Becque. And in the final chapter, "The Cemetery at Hoga Point," Michener comments on the fallen heroes. Given a tour of the cemetery, the narrator, exhausted by the assault on Kuralei, ponders the graves of his comrades. He is accompanied by two black American servicemen who enjoy the tranquillity of caring for the cemetery, particularly because their new commander is racially prejudiced and treats them poorly. Looking at the rows of crosses, the narrator laments that it has taken death to end all distinctions of race and rank: "There are no officers and men. There are only men." Michener later commented on the tenor of his final chapter: "If I had one purpose in writing, it was to extol the brotherhood we seem able to attain only in cemeteries."

After watching a movie each night on Santo, he would retire to his Quonset, pull out his sheaf of notes, pore over his photos, and until two or three in the morning he would work industriously on his book. "For whom did I write as I sat night after night fighting the mosquitoes with those little bombs of insecticide the Navy gave us and pecking out my stories on the typewriter? Not the general public, whom I did not care to impress; not the custodians of literature. . . . I wrote primarily for myself, to record the reality of World War II, and for the young men and women who had lived it." When he had six chapters written, he was brave enough to show them to a few fellow officers. "Christ, this stinks," a lieutenant barked. "Why don't you change it here and there?" Michener claimed the man depressed him so much that if he later had a bulldog he would name it after him.

Seeking some reassurance, he turned to his neighbor Fred, who promised Jim he would read a chapter and report back in the morning. Promptly at sunrise, Fred appeared in Jim's Quonset and announced that Michener's effort was "Not bad, not bad at all." Michener fed him chapter after chapter. No matter what the material, Fred's response was "Not bad at all" or "You know what you're doing."

"I cannot express how much I valued his support," confessed Michener, "for writing in an empty shed darkened with mighty shadows and infested with mosquitoes is a task that cries out for moral support, and he provided it."

•

Sometime between the end of February and the beginning of March 1945, Michener finished the draft of *Tales of the South Pacific*. He felt confident enough to contemplate sending it in its present state to Macmillan for possible publication.

Since leaving for active duty with the navy, Michener had remained on good terms with his employer. He corresponded periodically with George Brett, who as early as January 1944, just before Michener shipped out to the South Pacific, told Jim that "there is a big job to be done at Macmillan. I am satisfied that you have a good future with this company, and I am hoping to persuade you to take advantage of the first opportunity that comes along to come on back. You are needed here." The South Pacific, however, had changed Michener. He no longer had the allegiance to Macmillan and to an editorial career that he once had had. He occasionally sent Brett letters that he was still "very interested" in staying with company, but he would have to finish his active duty first.

The war, too, was dragging on, although an overwhelming American victory on Iwo Jima and the invasion of Okinawa suggested that the end was in sight. In truth, Michener was equivocating in his career path until he saw how his first book would be received. Just perhaps, the life of a writer with all of its alluring freedoms might await him, and he would stall Brett and Macmillan until time and circumstance proved otherwise.

To prevent any conflict of interest, Macmillan had an ironclad rule that it did not publish works by its employees. Reasoning that he was not presently a full-time employee of the company, Jim mailed his manuscript to Macmillan in New York but under an assumed name and "with a contrived return address to which the response could be sent. Under those devious conditions it was accepted."

Jim's immediate supervisor at Macmillan was Harold Latham, a no-nonsense senior editor who, according to Michener, "was an aloof scholar with a keen eye for the best-seller." Latham would be forever known as the man who discovered Margaret Mitchell and her blockbuster novel *Gone with the Wind*, a coup he never tired of relating to interested parties. When *Tales of the South Pacific* arrived on his desk, and after Michener's deception had been overcome, he consulted with George Brett on how best to approach the publication of Jim's book. Latham and Brett agreed that it needed further work. Brett proposed to circulate the manuscript to three of his toughest readers, who would make suggestions as to the work's merit and its ability to sell in the marketplace. Only after the readers had reported could the book proceed to publication.

In May 1945 George Brett wrote to Michener explaining this process. Brett feared that publishing *Tales* would ultimately drive Michener away from Macmillan, and he did not want lose one of his best editors. Indeed, in the back of Brett's mind was the possibility that someday Michener would make a fine executive for Macmillan Publishing.

For the name on the jacket of his first book Michener settled on James A. Michener—the A standing for his middle name Albert. Brett and Latham began addressing their letters to Michener in this fashion.

While Macmillan was deliberating the decision to publish and awaiting the readers' reports, Michener's naval career took a dramatic turn. In April 1945 the Allies swept across western Germany and awaited the unconditional German surrender. With victory in Europe only days away, American forces in the Pacific felt a surge of optimism that they were on the verge of winning their own war. In May, Lieutenant Michener was called to Nouméa, where he was offered the job of naval historian for the entire Pacific theater. The position meant a promotion to lieutenant commander, unlimited transportation to all the islands of the Pacific from New Zealand to Tarawa, from the Marquesas to Micronesia, and access to top-secret documents and high-level government officials. He would be working under the supervision of Samuel Eliot Morison, the esteemed Harvard professor of history. However, the assignment would lengthen his tour of duty in the South Pacific by six to eight months.

Michener as naval historian, interviewing troops on unnamed island in 1945. Courtesy Library of Congress.

The rear admiral who offered him the assignment expected that he might like some time to think it over, but Michener needed only a few minutes. Two things drove his decision to remain in the South Pacific: his epiphany on the Tontouta airstrip several months before, and the realization that his marriage was falling apart. "I really had no burning desire to get back home," he admitted to himself.

And so in early June, two months before the Americans dropped the atomic bomb on Hiroshima and Nagasaki, Lieutenant Commander James Michener began his assignment by initiating histories of Bora Bora and Tangatabu, and later supervised the writing of twelve other histories including those of Espíritu Santo, New Caledonia, Fiji, and Guadalcanal. The reports eventually ended up back in Washington, where they were scrutinized by the House Naval Affairs Committee. "Long after I'm dead," joked Michener, "somebody will find them gathering dust . . . and they'll be published as affectionate little records of the absurd."

While Jim was engaged in writing his histories of various islands—which ironically is the occupation he had already attributed to his book's narrator—Macmillan was busy combing his manuscript. In July Harold Latham reported that all three readers had responded favorably, but there were certain parts for Michener to revise. The most critical concern was Michener's characterizations. "You have imagined your characters indistinctly," wrote Latham, "with the result that in their various appearances they seem to be different people." He also expressed concern that Michener often resorted to melodrama, inappropriate humor, and philosophizing: "You have not acquired the skill to do this sort of thing and write this kind of conversation without becoming stilted and self-conscious." Latham encouraged Michener to revise the manuscript accordingly so that publication could proceed without delay.

But Michener did not respond to Latham's request until autumn, suggesting that he was deeply involved in researching, traveling, and writing histories for the navy. In November he wrote Latham that he agreed with "almost all of your criticisms," and he would begin revising the manuscript. George Brett was also breathing down his neck about returning to Macmillan, so Michener felt additional pressure to polish his book and secure his release from the navy. "We need you and we need you now," Brett urged in a letter.

In the meantime, the war in the Pacific had ended with the Japanese unconditional surrender on August 14, 1945. The operation to dismantle Santo as a military base was under way. At first the navy had debated how best to dispose of the massive amounts of military equipment on the base. There was insufficient deck space on ships heading to America, with priority given to returning servicemen. Moreover, it was speculated that if the equipment were returned to America it would drastically affect the economy, as no buyers would want to purchase new cars and trucks when they could cheaply get used army jeeps. The U.S. government offered to sell the surplus equipment to the French authorities, thereby keeping it for the locals on Santo. Reasoning that the American military would not be foolish enough to repatriate the equipment and would end up leaving most of it on the island anyway, the French did not respond.

After some delay with no resolution, the Americans acted. They lined up all the jeeps, bulldozers, ambulances, and other heavy equipment near the Segond Channel. The line stretched for three-quarters of a mile. Ignitions were switched on. Bricks were placed on accelerators as the equipment rumbled down a ramp into water forty feet deep. Desks and office furniture were also dumped there, including the desk and typewriter used by Michener to type his reports and his first book. Later the area became known as Million Dollar Point, and to this day it is a major diving attraction on Santo.

As Santo emptied out, Michener made his last revisions to *Tales of the South Pacific*. Although it would still undergo some copy editing by Macmillan, the book was now generally in the form in which it would be published in 1947. While awaiting his release from the navy, Michener packed it away in heavy paper, shoved it in his briefcase, and stuffed the briefcase in his duffel bag. In January he was officially discharged, and Lieutenant Commander James Michener boarded the USS *Kwajalein* for his return voyage to America.

CHAPTER 6

Tales of the South Pacific

The initial in-house readers of Michener's manuscript fell into two camps. The first camp enthusiastically declared it one of the most entertaining works to come out of the war, praising its comic sketches and its often risqué glimpses of military life behind the lines. The other group was just as vocal about its demerits, calling it shallow and a series of unconnected incidents that bore little or no relation to each other. To both sides Michener insisted that the book was written solely for him and the men and women who served in the South Pacific, and any attempt at a literary product was purely coincidental.

One of the strong supporters was Cecil Scott, a sharp-eyed Englishman in whose hands Macmillan placed the final editing of the manuscript. Scott went through *Tales* with a light pencil, replacing most of the sailor slang with more common usage. He did leave, however, Michener's unique narrative voice, one that reached out to the common man and to the sailor who had just returned from the war. It was a contrived voice, Scott decided, almost amateurish, but it enfolded Michener's characters in genuine understanding.

The seven stories that comprise the first third of *Tales* portray the characters preparing for the fictional Operation Alligator, which targets an island Michener calls Kuralei. In the elegiac opening chapter, "The South Pacific," the reader is introduced to Admiral Kester, the operational commander, and his nemesis, the notorious Lieutenant Tony Fry, who, along with Luther Billis in later chapters, smashes nearly every military regulation he can find. In the following chapter, "Coral Sea," Tony Fry appears as a recurring character with a group of Allied pilots and a marooned New Zealander during the naval battle of the Coral Sea. In "Mutiny," Fry further reveals his rebellious self by refusing to destroy an island monument standing in the way of a proposed American airstrip—the story that Michener heard at the Hotel de Gink months before.

In the ironically titled "An Officer and a Gentleman," Ensign Bill Harbison, a narcissistic married officer, is posted to Efate, a small island in the New Hebrides not far from Santo. As a kind of naval Richard Cory, he enjoys the duplicitous life on the island until the boredom and waiting begin to take their toll. He seeks affairs with several nurses stationed on the island, including the lovely Nellie Forbush of Otolousa, Arkansas. "Never in a hundred years would Bill Harbison have noticed in her the States," remarks the narrator. "But on the island of Efate where white women were the exception and pretty white women rarities, Nellie Forbush was a queen." Nellie falls for Harbison, who does not reveal his marital status. One night while drunk he tries to assault Nellie, who resists. After crushing Nellie's hopes with the admission that he is married, Harbison moves on to his next conquest and eventually leaves the Pacific theater, shipping home without seeing action.

By far the most dramatic and memorable story occurs in chapter 5, "The Cave," which relates the mysterious exploits of the British coastwatcher called simply the Remittance Man—an exile living on money sent from home. Lieutenant Tony Fry reappears in the story as the navy's front man in receiving the Remittance Man's radio transmissions. Day after day with few breaks, the coastwatcher broadcasts his weather reports and observations of troop movements in The Slot of the Solomon Islands. Fry and his men listen intently, passing along important information to Nouméa and but mostly feeding on the Remittance Man's buoyant reports. An unseen but deeply felt camaraderie develops between the coastwatcher and the American troops. The broadcasts proceed until the Remittance Man, eventually identified as a British trader named Anderson, is abruptly cut off. The Americans, fearing that the Japanese have discovered his whereabouts, become alarmed. When the Japanese finally quit the Solomons, Fry petitions his superiors to organize a search party, and they discover that Anderson has died brutally at the hands of the departing Japanese.

"The Milk Run" introduces the reader to Lieutenant Bus Adams, a navy bomber pilot, who bails out into the waters of The Slot without a life raft. While Adams bobs on the water, the navy mounts a comprehensive rescue effort that ends up costing the taxpayer $600,000. It is an exorbitant sum, as the rescued man concedes. "But it's sure worth every cent of the money. If you happen to be that pilot."

In the chapter "Alligator," which closes out the first third of *Tales*, plans for a massive strike on Kuralei are initiated by the Joint Chiefs of Staff. Soon the ripple effect begins to affect every base in the Pacific, as men prepare for the coming onslaught: "From Australia, New Zealand, the Aleutians, Pearl Harbor, Point Hueneme, and more than eight hundred other places, men slowly or speedily collected at appointed spots. Marines who were sweating and cursing in Suva would soon find themselves caught in gasping swirl which would end only upon the beach at Kuralei. . . ."

The physical and romantic heart of *Tales* is comprised of the next series of stories: "Our Heroine," "Dry Rot," "Fo' Dolla,'" "Passion," "A Boar's Tooth," and "Wine for the Mess at Segi." After transferring from Efate, Ensign Forbush begins her new assignment on Santo, where she is soon invited along with several military friends to the home of Emile de Becque. She begins a whirlwind, and later stormy, relationship with the French planter. We learn that de Becque has lived twenty-six years on the island. Originally from Marseilles, he fled France because he killed a man who was terrorizing the local population. On Santo, he built his copra plantation into one of the most successful in the New Hebrides. When the war came along, he proudly organized the Free French movement on Santo. He is also aware of the broadcasts of Anderson, the Remittance Man. For the most part, like Ratard, like de Becque.

As love engulfs Nellie and Emile, he asks her to marry him. While considering Emile's offer, she has dinner with Bus Adams, who accidentally divulges that de Becque has eight children by a succession of women: four of Emile's daughters are half Javanese, two are half Tonkinese, and two are half Polynesian. De Becque tries to convince Nellie that such liaisons are the cultural norm in the South Pacific. However, she wrestles with her deep-seated bigotry:

> Emile de Becque, not satisfied with Javanese and Tonkinese women, had also lived with a Polynesian. A nigger! To Nellie's tutored mind any person living or dead who was not white or yellow was a nigger. And beyond that no words could go! Her entire Arkansas upbringing made it impossible for her to deny the teachings of her youth. Emile de Becque had lived with the nigger. He had nigger children. If she married him, they would be her step-daughters.

Nellie breaks off with Emile, and in the ensuing turmoil searches her feelings for him, ultimately realizing that the reason she joined the navy was "to see the world" and "meet other people." She has come to the right place at the right time. She puts her prejudice aside and drives back to de Becque's home, where Nellie, Emile, and his daughters join in singing a French song.

"Dry Rot" relates the tale of Joe, a lonely sailor who builds unique contraptions out of the flotsam and jetsam found on his South Pacific "rock," including a shower rigged from huge GI gas cans. He is adopted by the rascally Luther Billis, a "big, fat, and brown" Seabee, "beautifully tattooed," who sets him up with lovelorn women back in the States.

In "Fo' Dolla'" Bloody Mary enters the fray by upsetting the naval base on Santo. She is organizing the local Tonkinese into abandoning their plantation jobs and selling grass skirts for "fo' dolla'" (pidgin for four dollars) to the troops, a situation that the military cannot tolerate. Marine lieutenant Joe Cable is assigned to monitor and neutralize the pesky Tonkinese woman. Mary soon entices Cable to the island of Bali Ha'i, sixteen miles offshore, where she introduces him to the lovely Liat, revealed to be her daughter. Against his better judgment, Cable and Liat enter into a torrid affair, even though he is engaged to a Pennsylvania girl back home.

Michener's Aoba—now transformed into Bali Ha'i—becomes a war-time sanctuary for Santo's women, who are sequestered there because of the influx of servicemen, an arrangement suggested by his visit to Mother Margaret's School for Girls. Bali Ha'i and Vanicoro, both off limits to the enlisted men of Santo, rise compellingly through the mists. The former symbolizes unspoiled paradise and sexual energy, the latter a place of savagery and cannibalistic rituals; together they are a metaphor for the virginal Liat and her blowzy Tonkinese mother. "Liat was the very spirit of Bali-ha'i," wrote Michener. "In the days to come that lovely statuette in brown marble was to be the magnet which would draw him back to the island time after time after time, like an echo from a distant life." When Bloody Mary suggests that Cable marry her daughter and remain in the Pacific after the war, Cable, like Nellie, searches his deepest soul for answers and, also like Nellie, feels the bitter divide of racial prejudice. But unlike Nellie, Cable can never bring together the two worlds of Main Line Philadelphia and Bali Ha'i, of Princeton University and a lush, sin-less paradise. Cable cannot stay with Liat as Melville could not stay on Nuku Hiva with Fayaway. "He could not go back," wrote D. H. Lawrence of Melville. Nor could Lawrence himself: "Back towards the past savage life. One cannot go back. It is one's destiny inside one. These people are not 'savages.' One does not despise them. One does not feel superior. But there is a gulf. There is a gulf in time and being. I cannot commingle my being with theirs." Michener understood the pain this brought, and he considered Cable's tragic parting from Liat the most poignant part of his book.

Ultimately Cable rejects both Bali Ha'i and Liat, for there is another calling more urgent and in line with his character: Operation Alligator is under way, and it soon enfolds him in its sweep. "In the morning Lt. Joe Cable, fully determined to be the best Marine officer in the coming strike, was up early. . . . He repacked his battle gear twice to make it ready for a landing. . . . He clenched his fist. 'It's good to be back in the swing,' he said to himself."

After the chapter "Passion" examines the duties of a navy censor poring over servicemen's letters home, Luther Billis returns in "A Boar's Tooth" to find the ultimate pig's tusk for his bracelet. Luther's jewelry provokes amazement among the fighting men of the South Pacific: "On his left arm Billis wore an aluminum watch band, a heavy silver slave bracelet with his name engraved, and a superb wire circlet made of woven airplane wire welded and hammered flat. On his right wrist he had a shining copper bracelet on which his social security and service numbers were engraved. And he wore a fine boar's tusk." The trouble is, Billis won't rest until he finds the most superior tusk in the New Hebrides, even larger than the one he has. Draped in jewelry, stenciled with tattoos, Billis heads to Vanicoro on an unauthorized voyage to find the object of his obsession.

As Billis so eloquently explains to his fellow Seabees, the pig has an honored place in South Pacific culture and the pig's tusk is a treasured amulet. The most prized tusk has a double curve and takes the pig years to grow. On the forbidding island that looms over Bali Ha'i, Billis witnesses the ritual killing of the pig and the removal of the sacred tusk.

"Wine for the Mess at Segi" finds the ubiquitous Tony Fry provoking calamity, defying authority, but avoiding total insubordination. This time he is in charge of the mess hall on Segi Point in the Solomons. Realizing that he is running low on Christmas cheer for the holiday season, he enlists the aid of pilot Bus Adams. In a madcap mission in Adams's plane the *Bouncing Belch*, Fry and Adams hop from the Solomons to Nouméa and score some twenty cases of liquor. They bring the liquor back intact, but not the plane.

The remaining third of *Tales of the South Pacific* focuses on the marines, sailors, and soldiers involved in the invasion of Kuralei, and the tone shifts from the personal to the more gritty aspects of military action: troop deployments, naval maneuvers, and last-minute training for the beach assault. In "The Airstrip at Konora," "Those Who Fraternize," "The Strike," "Frisco," "The Landing on Kuralei," and "The Cemetery at Hoga Point," interminable boredom is supplanted by the swirl of battle. There are still moments of levity, however, as in one sequence Luther Billis abandons his post to hunt for Japanese samurai swords as souvenirs. We learn that Tony Fry and Lieutenant Cable have both been killed, as have nearly three hundred American servicemen who lie under the rows of white crosses on Hoga Point.

Guided by two black GIs, the narrator, now bitter and demoralized by the battle for Kuralei, wanders among the crosses on a promontory overlooking the Pacific. He speculates on who will replace these strong, valiant men. "Throughout the Pacific, in Russia, in Africa, and soon on fronts not yet named," he laments, "good men were dying. Who would take their place? Who would marry the girls they would have married? Or build the buildings they would have built?"

He worries that men like the fallen Commander Hoag would be replaced by incompetent bigots and racists. "He was from Atlanta," the narrator remarks, "but he championed the Negro. He was a rich man, but he befriended his meanest enlisted man. He was a gentile, but he placed Jews in positions of command. . . . Yet when he died a loud-mouthed bully came along to take his place." At this point, the narrator/Michener is concerned with a much larger question: Will the postwar world further descend into the darkness of hatred and prejudice, or will a few good men survive to champion democracy and egalitarianism? Will there be a enough brave men left after Kuralei, Iwo Jima, Tarawa, Okinawa, Guam, Bougainville, Corregidor, Tulagi, and Guadalcanal to rescue and fight for the rights of man?

•

But do all these scenes and characters constitute a novel? Or are they simply a grouping of tales adding up to a short story collection? A good case can be made for either view. Virtually from the day that Michener's book arrived at Macmillan, editors and readers debated this point. The unusual structure and narrative voice confounded critics and readers even after publication.

Michener himself always had a definite idea about how *Tales* should be defined: "This is not a standard novel and could not be handled in a standard way. What did work was a loose collection of delicately interrelated stories in which no one character, no one setting, and no one concept assumed priority. War is sloppy. Men move in and out of relationships. And in the end things drift apart."

Does Michener suggest that, since war is sloppy, a book can reflect that sloppiness? The answer is yes. *Tales* is essentially an existential novel. It is about fragmentation, unresolved conflicts, momentary gain, and lives left dangling. Trying to deal with intolerable reality, a diverse group of military personnnel struggle with the moment. War always lurks like a dark, unseen force beyond the island. The threat of war shapes everything, including character. Humor conquers despair; action displaces longing and fear. Luther Billis chases the ultimate boar's tusk as if he is after the Medal of Honor. But medals are for heroes, and there are few heroes in Michener's war. Admirals and commanders behave as foolishly as enlisted men. All characters are leveled and made frighteningly vulnerable.

Michener felt a degree of guilt over the eventual success of his first work. Writing in the 1970s to a friend, he said: "The saddest experience a man like me can have is to know a really fine young writer who writes a good, solid first novel and by some miracle gets it published. He then watches the newspapers, and not one, not even the third echelon reviews it. He waits in vain. Your heart can ache for such a friend." Later in the same letter he added: "Pretty surely I couldn't get *Tales of the South Pacific* published today. Couldn't even get it published. So I am not being mock-modest when I say that I have known quite a few young men who can write better than I can who never had the breaks. Not even one break."

PART II

On Broadway

Coming Home

After celebrating his thirty-ninth birthday in early February 1946, Lieutenant Commander James A. Michener, United States Navy Reserve, sat at
his desk in Macmillan's spacious first floor, staring at a pile of manuscripts
that were proposed textbooks in the history and literature fields. Espíritu
Santo it was not. Guadalcanal it was not. Aggie Grey's Cosmopolitan Club
in Samoa it was not. And the boundless Pacific with its strings of pearls
called islands it was certainly not. Still, glancing around him as typewrit-
ers clacked away and editors buzzed by him and disappeared into their
offices, he felt that at least he was at a secure job, and that the greatness
he promised himself to pursue on the Tontouta airstrip he might be able
to attain here.

He was treated as something of a war hero by his coworkers. A few
stopped by his desk to cajole him into telling of his experiences in the
South Pacific. Although he filled them in on the doings on Guadalcanal
at the Hotel de Gink and on Bora Bora, he was also quick to remind them
he saw little action. The fact that Michener had a book about the war to
be published by Macmillan was also cause for some rousing conversation
by the water cooler.

Three years in the navy, two in the South Pacific, had changed Michener,
made him more mature and ready to take on more difficult assignments.
His hairline had receded, and his hair was shorn to cocoa brown stubble.
His round wire-rimmed glasses accentuated his protruding nose. At five
foot ten, he walked with the rolling gait of a sailor.

In mid-February Macmillan, in the person of Harold Latham, offered

Jim a contract for *Tales of the South Pacific*, carrying with it a $500 advance against royalties plus serialization rights. The book would be put on the fall list, with an early November publication date.

Lady Luck always seemed to court Michener. It happened many times during his academic career, it happened when he was offered his assignments in the South Pacific, and it happened during the three airplane mishaps (two crashes) in his lifetime. Lady Luck returned again when the *Saturday Evening Post* offered $4,000 for the serial rights to two of his stories from *Tales*. It was an enormous sum for a man who had walked around with holes in his shoes for much of his life. The *Post* offer also meant that Macmillan would delay book publication until February 1947, a move that did not bother Latham, Michener, or George Brett, since it would give *Tales* more reader exposure and publicity.

In December 1946 and January 1947 the *Post* published "The Cave" (retitled "The Remittance Man") and "The Airstrip at Konora" (retitled "Best Man in de Navy"). The *Post* introduced the author Michener and his "extraordinary book," a book that the magazine's editors claimed captured "the what-it-was-really-like flavor of the war" better than anything yet written.

Initially the magazine's readers wondered if Michener was relating fact or fiction in his stories. His spare, journalistic style, his ability to capture local color and incident, appealed to readers seeking an authentic voice from the war. One reader wrote Michener: "You put in words what it was really like out there even in the good days when I was there . . . you really have it, that indefinable 'feel' of the situations and the people, especially the people." Such letters made Michener swell with pride: he had gotten down on paper the truth of the war in the private and public lives of the men and women who served. He hoped his book would be a best seller, but it meant more to him that he had first touched the lives of ordinary Americans.

·

In the months following his return to New York, Michener's private life was, at best, unsettled. His wife Patti had also been mustered out of the army and was living across town in Manhattan. They did not live together upon her return, but saw each other only to confirm that their marriage was over. Patti packed her things and returned to South Carolina, never to see Jim again. Although there were many parts to their discord, Michener blamed the war for their marriage's failure. "I don't hate," Michener once

Michener in 1948 after winning the Pulitzer Prize for fiction. Courtesy Library of Congress.

said, "but I do amputate." It became characteristic of Michener to end any relationship that was not working for him, and to leave no opening for a reunion.

Besides, New York and all its postwar excitement was at his doorstep. He rented a one-room apartment on West Twelfth Street, not far from his office. Always tight with money, the result of a difficult childhood, he lugged in a portable oven and grill to cut down on expenses. He set up his hi-fi equipment in the corner and it was usually playing Brahms or Beethoven. He was usually up at four in the morning working on his new book, a semiautobiographical novel based on his own maturation in Pennsylvania and New York, tentatively titled *The Homeward Journey*. In the months before *Tales* appeared in bookstores, Michener kept a regular schedule of writing early in the morning, heading off to work at seven-thirty, and spending a relaxing evening at the opera or theater.

He became reacquainted with his boyhood home in Doylestown, Pennsylvania, as if to coax out the memories of his childhood while he worked on the novel. He had been an infrequent visitor to Doylestown over the years, but in summer 1946 he was a steady weekend guest. Often he left Manhattan by car Friday evening, headed southwest on the highway through New Jersey, crossed the Delaware River, and was in Doylestown by nightfall. The quaint and provincial town of his youth spoke to his citified soul. In the postwar years, however, Doylestown and Bucks County had changed drastically. As a bedroom community of New York, it had blossomed into a mecca for artists and writers. The novelist James Gould Cozzens lived just across the river in Lambertville, New Jersey; in northern Bucks County the Nobel Prize winner Pearl Buck resided; and only three miles from the heart of Doylestown, Oscar Hammerstein II, the noted librettist and musical teammate of Richard Rodgers, lived on a patrician and neatly manicured parcel of land called Highland Farm. Despite its Manhattan invasion, Doylestown still wore the look of a colonial town.

•

With the breakup of his marriage and the often rocky adjustment to civilian life, Michener sought escape in the musical theater. In mid-May 1946 he attended an opening-week performance of *Annie Get Your Gun*, a vibrant production written by Herbert and Dorothy Fields, with songs by Irving Berlin, and produced by the Broadway icons Richard Rodgers and Oscar Hammerstein. It starred the electric Ethel Merman, whose belting out of "There's No Business Like Show Business" delighted Michener. The production was directed by Joshua Logan—Captain Joshua Logan, United States Army, actually—who, like Jim, had been released from active duty less than a year before. Unbeknownst to Michener, both Logan and Richard Rodgers were in the house that night, carefully watching the crowd's reaction to the performers.

Josh Logan shared many qualities with James Michener, introspection not being one of them. Logan was born in 1908, a year after Michener, in Texarkana, Texas. He was raised in Shreveport, Louisiana, and graduated from Princeton University, where he distinguished himself as an actor and director of the University Players. He was voluble, excitable, and suffered from a bipolar disorder that hospitalized him in the middle of his burgeoning career. Although this nervous disorder troubled him throughout his life, he frequently joked about it, once calling himself "as sound as a nut" to an army doctor.

Logan first teamed with Richard Rodgers and Lorenz Hart on the 1938 Broadway production of *I Married an Angel*. In 1940 Logan directed and coauthored Rodgers and Hart's *Higher and Higher*; in 1942 he reprised his directorial role in Rodgers and Hart's *By Jupiter*. That same year he was drafted into the army.

Logan insisted that he wanted no part of a desk job, but opted instead for a combat assignment. While he could have easily exploited his celebrity status, he chose to be "one of the guys." Upon entering the army as a captain, he wanted to prove to himself that he was something more than a Broadway showman. "I had talked my way through every school I'd gone to," he wrote. "I'd pretended, cheated, lied, said I'd read books I'd never opened, repeated remarks of others as my own. But now was the time to end all that fakery." The army—and perhaps his own imminent death— would reveal the truth about him. "And maybe I'd find out soon."

After training at Camp Mackall in North Carolina, he was transferred as an intelligence officer to Lancashire in northern England and then, in the days prior to the invasion of Normandy, to Upottery airbase in Devonshire. Huge maps of Europe papered the room as high-ranking officers discussed strategies for D-day. Captain Logan's assignment included briefing pilots who would drop airborne troops on German positions near the French town of Sainte-Mère-Eglise. In his memoir Logan recalled the eve of the landing: "There was a final pilot briefing at seven. As the pilots filed in, they looked like sober schoolboys going to class." Later Logan watched as the paratroopers were loaded into the planes that would begin the assault wave. "They had blackened faces so they'd be harder to see at night. Each soldier was in battle dress that had been sprayed with antigas liquid, giving him a wild mottled appearance, had pockets bulging with grenades and bullet clips, and a pistol pushed within his belt. Some stuck their chewing gum on the plane's wing for good luck."

It was only after the Normandy invasion, when the planes returned, that Logan and the other officers learned the tragic story: the weather was terrible; only a few of the planes made it to the drop zones, and they unloaded the airborne troops blindly into unlit enemy positions; most were captured or fell helplessly into the sea. "The infantry would be landing from boats in a few hours on the French beaches dubbed Omaha and Utah. They would be counting—and mostly in vain—on our paratroopers to clear out Germans and secure vital bridges."

While James Michener was encountering the endless longing and waiting in the South Pacific, Captain Josh Logan was feeling the helplessness, the utter futility of trying to pull off a successful operation with a minimal loss of life. However, it was this bond, this gentle understanding between them forged on the beaches of Normandy and in the jungles of New

Guinea, that eventually sweetened their friendship and made them such fierce comrades.

Logan served the remainder of the war as a publications officer in Paris. In November 1945 he returned home, fretting about his uncertain future. "Who would now want a doddering thirty-seven-year-old has-been," he lamented. "There must be hundreds of cheap and young directors coming back from the service. How could there be jobs for all of us?" There was, however, a new musical about Annie Oakley, *Annie Get Your Gun*, just going into production that autumn. It would have as its composer the venerable Jerome Kern, as its producer Logan's old collaborator Richard Rodgers, and as its director, if Rodgers had his way, Logan. And what Rodgers wanted, he usually got.

Rodgers by then was something of a Broadway phenomenon. In 1943, after the untimely death of Lorenz Hart from acute alcoholism, Rodgers teamed with fellow Columbia grad Oscar Hammerstein II. Together they revolutionized musical theater, first with the landmark *Oklahoma!* in 1943 and then with the magisterial *Carousel* in 1945. *Oklahoma!* won a special Pulitzer Prize and continued its run into 1944 and beyond. It was so successful that a special USO show played to more than a million troops overseas.

Carousel entered Rodgers and Hammerstein's world in strange fashion. In 1944 the Theatre Guild asked the team to adapt the Hungarian Ferenc Molnár's drama *Liliom*, which had a successful Broadway run in the 1920s. Both partners had difficulty with its setting and scope. The play featured a carousel barker, a chest-beating bully who makes everyone unhappy and returns from the dead to haunt his adolescent daughter. Moreover, the play was set in Hungary—not exactly the territory that Rodgers and Hammerstein preferred.

But their determination to stage a successful musical overcame their doubts, and by resetting the play in turn-of-the-century New England, they Americanized the staging and broadened its appeal. Rodgers ended up preferring it to all of his and Hammerstein's productions. It was at first thought that a play dealing with faith would have a difficult time with audiences. But the war in Europe and the Pacific actually boosted the appeal to faith and the result was an enthusiastic wartime turnout for the show.

In 1945 Rodgers and Hammerstein paired for the filming of *State Fair*, a corn-stuffed piece of Americana served up to war-weary audiences, for which they won an Oscar for the song "It Might As Well Be Spring." It was the only time a person named Oscar won an Oscar. As the war finally ended, Rodgers and Hammerstein were the kings of New York.

When *Annie Get Your Gun* came along, similar success was not only planned, it was banked on. Rodgers believed that Joshua Logan's talent for direction would give the show its zest and enthusiasm. Therefore, when Logan telephoned Rodgers that he was about to be discharged from the army, Rodgers was overjoyed. But there was a tragic caveat.

"Josh, the show is falling apart," moaned Rodgers. "Jerome Kern is terribly ill. The doctors think he might die tonight." Kern had collapsed while walking near Central Park and was in critical condition. Feeling that he had hung all his aspirations on *Annie*, Logan fell into a brief depression. When Kern died a short time later, Logan waited for the verdict on the show.

The principals talked over possible replacements for Kern. Predictably, the name of Irving Berlin came up first. Berlin was, like Kern, a legendary figure on Broadway. He was also notoriously demanding. He'd never do it, was the consensus, unless he had total control.

"Wait a minute," said Hammerstein. "I don't think you should eliminate him until you've asked him."

After some gentle arm-twisting, Berlin welcomed the idea, even though he claimed that *Annie* was on the face of it "hillbilly music." He went right to work creating some of the most memorable songs in musical theater, including "They Say It's Wonderful," "Anything You Can Do," and the showstopper "There's No Business Like Show Business," which became emblematic of the American theater.

For director Joshua Logan, *Annie Get Your Gun* proved that he was no "doddering has-been" but a force to be reckoned with for years to come on the boards of Broadway.

•

Heading into the fall of 1946, Rodgers and Hammerstein resisted the temptation to have each new show outshine the previous one. Such was the case with the low-voltage productions of *Happy Birthday* in October and *John Loves Mary* in February 1947. *Happy Birthday*, written by Anita Loos and directed by Josh Logan, featured Helen Hayes in the starring role. *John Loves Mary* was a light comedy that, if not for Logan's sound and inventive direction, would have been savaged by the critics. Neither play approached the success of *Oklahoma!*, *Carousel*, or *Annie Get Your Gun*, but they indicated that Rodgers and Hammerstein—often called just R&H—were primarily more interested in solid production values than in the glitter of new shows.

Their partnership, characterized by harmony and mutual respect, was the envy of any creative team. The supremely gifted Rodgers was the administrative and business whiz of the collaboration. Generally it was Rodgers, or his lawyers, who negotiated with authors for the rights to their work. At cocktail parties, he would be the front man for the team, identifying important writers and production people to bring under their wing. As a graduate of the Juilliard School and a veteran of numerous Broadway musicals, he was one of the foremost musical talents in America. Possessed of a near-Mozartean gift for creating varied melodies, he could develop a memorable theme in no time, much to the chagrin of Hammerstein, who frequently labored over his lyrics. Hammerstein said that he was afraid to give Rodgers a lyric at a party because Rodgers would rush off to another room and start composing music to it. Aloof and sometimes frosty in manner, Rodgers was never much at home at social gatherings, preferring to sit at the piano while he chatted with adoring fans.

Oscar Hammerstein was a lovable bear of a man. "His warmth was so apparent," wrote Josh Logan, "it was hard to see the glints of steel in his eyes." Hammerstein developed the method of writing the lyrics first and then bringing them to Rodgers to write the score around them. Using this method, which worked time and time again, Rodgers and Hammerstein followed in the tradition of Gilbert and Sullivan, who pioneered the technique. Hammerstein usually wrote at his farm in Doylestown or his apartment in New York. His favorite position for creating was standing up or reclining on a sofa with numerous pillows tucked under him.

Hammerstein's lyrics were usually characterized by simple and uncomplicated phrases patterned after everyday speech. Although Oscar was not a musician, Rodgers discovered that he had "a superb sense of form" and knew a song's "architecture." Hammerstein stressed that the opening of a show is what makes or breaks or it; the opening lyrics have be arresting and magnificent. "If you start with the right opening," Hammerstein claimed, "you can ride for forty-five minutes on the telephone book. On the other hand, if you start off with a wrong one, it's an uphill fight all the way." In song construction, he believed, "everything should develop, every word should count, nothing should be reiterated or repeated unless you're doing it for effect."

He once coached the precocious Stephen Sondheim in the finer points of songwriting. "Don't imitate other people's emotions," he told the fifteen-year-old. "Speak your own." When the youth wrote of the wind and birds, trying to imitate the master, Oscar said: "You know, you don't believe in any of this stuff. Write what you feel. Don't write what *I* feel. I really believe all this stuff. *You* don't. If you write what you believe, you'll be ninety percent ahead of all other songwriters." Oscar went on to emphasize that in songwriting "the thought counts more than the rhyme." Rhyme, Hammerstein insisted, is easy. Expressing a clear, profound thought is the hard part and is the sum of the lyricist's art.

Sondheim admits he had a "snotty" attitude toward learning. When Hammerstein said one of his lyrics "doesn't say anything," Sondheim responded: "Well, what does 'Oh, What a Beautiful Mornin'' say?" To which Oscar replied, "Oh, it says a lot."

Still a schoolboy, Sondheim believed that to "say something" meant reduction to a pithy phrase, a neat answer on a test paper. However, for Oscar, the "something" did not have to be a philosophical truth but just an experience common to human beings. Hammerstein then encouraged the boy with a four-part assignment to be accomplished over the next few years. First, Sondheim should take a play he admired and make a musical out of it. Second, he should take an inferior play and try to fix its flaws while making a musical out of it. Third, he should adapt something nontheatrical, a novel or a short story, for the musical stage. And finally, he should write an original musical, creating the book and lyrics himself. "By the time you get through that," Hammerstein concluded, "you'll know something of what we've been talking about."

Taking each step as assigned by Oscar, Sondheim labored away while at Williams College. At the age of twenty-three and with his four musicals completed, Sondheim was prepared to take on the rigors of Broadway. It was only a matter of time before he blazed his own path in musical theater, writing and cowriting hits like *West Side Story*, *Gypsy*, *Company*, *Follies*, *A Little Night Music*, *Sweeney Todd*, *Sunday in the Park with George*, and *Into the Woods*.

While he was mentoring Sondheim, Hammerstein had his own ideas about writing and producing an original musical with Richard Rodgers. He envisioned telling a tale of a man from birth to death, a man assaulted by attacks on his personal integrity and seduced by worldly values. He would employ a Greek chorus and strip the setting bare, much like Thornton Wilder's *Our Town*. And like Wilder's play, it could be staged by colleges and universities, adding to its universal appeal. That was his intention in late 1946, but these were just vague sketches in his mind.

Much more tangible were his successes still on Broadway and for which the public was still singing his praises: *Oklahoma!* was in its fourth year at the St. James Theater; *Carousel* was at the Majestic; the indestructible *Show Boat*, which Hammerstein cowrote with Jerome Kern in 1927, was entrenched at the Ziegfeld; and *Annie Get Your Gun*, the youngster in the bunch, was at the Imperial Theatre.

"An Ugly, Monstrous Book"

Early in 1947, Cecil Scott handed Michener an advance copy of *Tales of the South Pacific*. The author had waited more than two years to see the book in print, but now that it had happened, Michener winced in pain. On the cover was a crude illustration of a nondescript island, seen in a bird's-eye view, with what resembled a navy destroyer plying the waters around its coast. With so many colorful and vivid scenes to choose from, the artist had selected one of the dullest. The insides were no better. "Wartime restrictions concerning paper required the use of the tag-end lot of a bizarre paper that was extremely thin," noted Michener, "and had two radically different surfaces front and back, as well as a dirty brownish coloring." As Michener thumbed the pages, Scott sheepishly muttered: "I did the best I could." It was not Scott's fault or Macmillan's, but the postwar shortage of quality paper. "It was an ugly, monstrous book," Michener declared, "a disgrace to a self-respecting company and a humiliation to its author."

Moreover, Macmillan had spent virtually nothing on promotion. Senior editors expected *Tales* to sell modestly but not in great numbers. One possible reason for its lack of marketing was that war books were risky ventures. The country yearned to "get out of uniform" and return to the business of living. Still, the *Post's* advance publication of two stories boosted initial sales. Although it was never a best seller, *Tales* went through two printings in the first six months. "It enjoyed a faltering life of about three weeks," Michener observed, "but in that brief period, it proved that a book does not have to garner a huge audience in order to succeed ultimately."

Michener was fortunate that his first book found its way into the critical press. Some journals and daily newspapers ignored it entirely. Michener himself predicted it "isn't going to create a big stir," though he felt "it is going to do better than we thought a war book could do." Several important critics, however, lifted it to initial stardom.

On Sunday, February second, the all-important *New York Times Book Review* ran a long piece titled "Atolls of the Sun" in which David Dempsey pronounced *Tales* "truly one of the most remarkable books to come out of the war in a long time." While he thought some of the stories ran too long, "even when he is uneconomical, Mr. Michener is never dull." Dempsey credited this "born story teller" with "a rare gift for human characterization and a wonderful command of dialogue" and concluded that "the line of men from the States to Mr. Michener's climactic battle was a long line. We are fortunate that Mr. Michener was in it."

The next morning the principal book critic of the daily *Times*, Orville Prescott, a Pulitzer Prize juror in fiction, wrote that *Tales* was "a substantial achievement which will make Mr. Michener famous. If it doesn't there is no such thing as literary justice. It is original in its material and point of view, fresh, simple and expert in its presentation, humorous, engrossing and surprisingly moving . . . appealing to mature and thoughtful minds while at the same time being vastly entertaining." Prescott seconded Dempsey, calling *Tales* "one of the best works of fiction yet to come out of the war."

John Cournos, writing in the *New York Sun*, declared *Tales* was "a pleasure as well as an education," marrying readability and action with "a general picture of war as it was fought in the South Pacific." Cournos found Michener "above all, adept at describing character."

Although most of the criticism was glowing, the book took its share of drubbing, especially from veterans. One such letter from a Commander C. A. Whyte, who had served in the South Pacific, informed the *Saturday Evening Post* that "Michener's trash nauseated me. It was about as far from a true story as anything I have ever read, and I may add, experienced."

The book that *Tales of the South Pacific* was frequently compared to (and that some claimed hobbled it) was Thomas Heggen's 1946 novel *Mister Roberts*. Like James Michener, Thomas Heggen was stationed in the South Pacific, and he saw limited action on Okinawa and Iwo Jima.

Mister Roberts focused on the average sailor and, in Heggen's words, was a tale that meandered "from apathy to tedium with occasional sidetrips to monotony and ennui." Mister Roberts, a lieutenant junior grade, is a well-educated officer stuck on a navy ship chafing for some action. He and assorted crew members are helpless victims of a tyrannical captain, who spurns most of Roberts's attempts to gain privileges for his men. To the men Roberts is a hero, and when he dies in battle, he becomes an inspiration to his shipmates.

Talented but self-destructive, Thomas Heggen wrote his first and only novel at the age of twenty-seven. Unlike *Tales*, it was a commercial and critical success. Unprepared for the adulation, Heggen stumbled into public forums trying to stimulate sales, but trembled before the literary audiences he attracted. Once in Boston, when the book had been out only a month but was selling briskly, he attended a book signing where a group of proper, blue-blooded women had assembled to hear him speak and answer questions. One polite lady asked, "Mr. Heggen, how did you happen to write this book?" Tom scratched his shock of unruly hair. "Well, shit, I was on the boat," he replied. From then on, the publisher kept Heggen on a short lead.

•

In the meantime, Joshua Logan was just finishing his directorial duties on *John Loves Mary* at the Booth Theatre and was looking about for new prospects. He had recently been offered Tennessee Williams's new play, *A Streetcar Named Desire*—and then lost the job when the author picked another director, Elia Kazan. "*Streetcar* was the best play I had read in years; maybe the best play I had ever read," Logan lamented. He passed several days in misery, and then his wife suggested he look again at *Mister Roberts* with idea of staging it. Both loved the book and thought it could make great theater. The problem was that Heggen's novel—much like *Tales of the South Pacific*—was loosely organized and episodic, with no real dramatic center. But the characters had genuine freshness and the comic situations seemed meant for the stage.

After he had negotiated the dramatic rights, Logan brought noted Broadway producer Leland Hayward into the project. With Hayward's backing, Logan set about to cowrite, along with Tom Heggen, the script that would transform the novel into a Broadway play. Heggen soon moved into Logan's Connecticut home and they began the tedious, often volatile, process of collaborative scriptwriting. Logan told Heggen outright: "I really love and respect this book, Tom, and we're going to have to work hard to keep a play close to your book."

For four solid months, Logan and Heggen labored on the script in Logan's living room. Heggen preferred to work at night, so the work began at five in the afternoon and lasted until the wee hours of the morning. Logan's wife Nedda became their sounding board. "We would wake her politely," wrote Logan, "and read her each new scene. She heard most of the play with her eyes closed, nodding affirmation, but delicately, so as not to nod herself awake." Their different personalities often clashed. "As brilliant as he was at the typewriter, Tom was incapable of sending out his laundry or of buying toothpaste. He found the world unkind in demanding cleanliness and other orderly pursuits."

When they had finished most of the play, they sought the approval of their producer, Leland Hayward. Josh read it to him page by page. Afterward Leland said, "Well, it's probably the greatest play that's ever been written in the history of the world, that's all!"

"What about Aristophanes?" asked Heggen.

"Aristophanes could never have written as good a play as that."

Logan and Heggen now entered the casting phase, which proved arduous because so many veterans thought the show was made for them. At the first casting call, more than eight hundred aspiring actors arrived at the Alvin Theatre. Eventually the role of the eponymous Mister Roberts was won by Henry Fonda, while Ensign Pulver, his harried adjutant, went to David Wayne.

•

Across town at the Majestic Theatre, Rodgers and Hammerstein were in the grip of their own exciting new project, their first original production, *Allegro*. What Hammerstein had envisioned at the end of 1946—the tale of an angst-ridden postwar everyman named Joe Taylor—was now ready to hit Broadway on October 10, 1947. Production and promotion costs were monumental; expectations were stratospheric. R&H hired Agnes de Mille to direct and choreograph the show. The sets were created by Jo Mielziner, who had established himself as one of Broadway's premier avant-garde designers. But for all its available talent and creativity, *Allegro's* simple allegory was crushed by the weight of the lush, overly wrought production. Mielziner's sets were complex systems of platforms, treadmills, staircases, pendulum stages, curtains, and loudspeakers. The cast was unwieldy, with forty-one principal and a hundred-odd secondary roles. Actors sang, danced, and jostled on the complex set, tending to diminish to the flow of the story line.

Although *Allegro* ran for nearly four hundred performances and won several Donaldson Awards, Rodgers and Hammerstein considered it a failure. Critics were divided on its merits and defects. Some were enamored of its innovative theater; others deplored the subordination of plot to pyrotechnics. Mixed opinions among critics and theatergoers might be acceptable for other writers, but not for Rodgers and Hammerstein. They had soaring hopes for *Allegro*, but, as the crowds that gathered on the dock and waved as the *Titanic* sailed away on her maiden voyage proved, great expectations mean very little in the long run.

In the bitter aftermath of *Allegro*, Rodgers and Hammerstein never again attempted to bring innovation to the theater. Instead they returned to what they did better than anyone else: adapting popular and obscure literary works for the musical stage.

•

Losing the chance to direct *A Streetcar Named Desire* always nettled Logan, but it did not deter him from attending the premiere on December 3, 1947, at the invitation of its designer, Jo Mielziner. After the show Logan and his wife went to Sardi's, Broadway's most famous watering hole, along with Mielziner and his brother, Kenneth MacKenna, who was a story editor at Metro-Goldwyn-Mayer. The conversation soon turned to *Mister Roberts*, scheduled for a February 1948 debut, of which Logan was justly proud. MacKenna told Logan that he had just finished considering a tale also set in the South Pacific, which he and other film companies had rejected. It had no dramatic possibilities, according to MacKenna, but Logan "might glean something from it—some color for *Mister Roberts*." The book was *Tales of the South Pacific*, by James Michener. Logan had heard of neither the book nor the author, but as he was about to leave for a vacation in Miami Beach, he bought a paperback copy and slipped it into his luggage.

At his hotel he skimmed through *Tales*, then spent some time with "Fo' Dolla,'" which he confessed "ensnared" him. He interested Leland Hayward in the book, and they both thought it would make a fabulous musical. Logan immediately said Rodgers and Hammerstein would be perfect for the property.

"Of course," Hayward agreed, "but don't you dare mention it to them. They'll want the whole goddamn thing. They'd gobble us up for breakfast!"

In his mind Logan built a beautiful scenario: Hayward would produce, Logan would direct, Rodgers would write the music, and Hammerstein would provide the book and lyrics. It was an elegant plan. But, Hayward reminded Logan, no one had yet secured the dramatic rights to *Tales of the South Pacific*. Logan agreed to move carefully, but at a cocktail party back in New York, perhaps pumped with a few extra drinks, he let slip to Richard Rodgers that he owned a story that would be perfect for the famous team. Rodgers scribbled himself a memo: "T of the S. Pacific—Fo' Dolla." Logan knew there was a chance that Rodgers and Hammerstein might eliminate him and Hayward from the show entirely. But he also knew that without R&H there could be no show at all.

It was not until late January 1948, nearly two months after Logan first read *Tales* in Florida, that Oscar Hammerstein read the book and became wildly enthusiastic. He and Rodgers agreed to coproduce with Logan and Hayward—but on their terms. R&H insisted on 51 percent of the proceeds, a proviso that infuriated both Logan and Hayward. However, the verbal deal was approved. The next step was to track down the unsung author, James Michener.

A Kid from Doylestown

During its first year of publication, *Tales of the South Pacific* enjoyed an encouraging but unspectacular journey. Through the spring, buoyed by positive reviews, it had a large spike in sales, but the following months saw a leveling off, so that by February 1948 it looked to be headed, like so many first novels, for literary obscurity.

Literary agents courted Michener throughout this period. Leading the way was Jacques Chambron, a descendant of the Marquis de Lafayette and agent for W. Somerset Maugham. Michener, at first dazzled by Chambron, was even more impressed by the next candidate, the dean of American literary agents, Carl Brandt Sr. Brandt offered Michener an attractive literary future if he could produce, and by "produce" Brandt meant quitting his job and devoting himself full time to writing. "I can't turn a poor writer into a good one," said Brandt, "and I can't suddenly rejuvenate a writer who's lost his touch. But what I can do is orchestrate a productive career and protect you in all your business relationships." At the time, Michener was neither emotionally nor financially able to quit his job at Macmillan. But he did send Brandt his newly completed manuscript, now retitled *The Fires of Spring*, in hopes that Brandt would accept him anyway.

In the meantime, another offer was dropped in Michener's lap. Leland Hayward called his office, wanting to present an important business opportunity. Over lunch Hayward acquainted Michener with the high hopes that *Tales* had generated among his Broadway cronies, and said Rodgers and Hammerstein were interested in buying the rights. Hayward offered five hundred dollars outright. Michener, however, was cautious, as "my rough childhood and jobs I had held in my teens that involved large sums had taught me a good deal about financing." He told Hayward: "Never an outright sale. Only royalties."

Hayward arranged for Michener to meet with Logan, Rodgers, and Hammerstein. It was at this meeting that Michener learned that he and Oscar were actually neighbors, living within a stone's throw of each other in Doylestown. But mainly Rodgers talked business, offering Michener 1 percent of the gross receipts from the proposed, as yet untitled, musical. Some possible titles were mentioned—Hammerstein at first thought it might be called *Operation Alligator* or simply *Alligator*, but these ideas were eventually dropped. R&H's lawyer, Howard Reinheimer, steered the agreement by suggesting to Michener that his book had no story line, no dramatic impact. "We couldn't possibly pay you what we did Lynn Riggs for his *Green Grow the Lilacs*, which *Oklahoma!* was based on. That was a real play. It had structure." Michener learned that Riggs received 1.5 percent of the box office for *Oklahoma!* In the end he accepted Reinheimer's offer of 1 percent and "never had regrets."

During the preproduction sessions on *South Pacific*, Michener mainly dealt with Hammerstein. Rodgers, however, was curious about some of the ramifications of the subject matter and locale. "Jim," he asked Michener, "do I have to use wailing guitars and ukuleles?"

Michener responded: "The only musical instrument I ever heard the natives play was two clubs beating the hell out of a gasoline drum."

Rodgers exhaled. "Thanks. I hate guitars."

•

Tom Heggen's *Mister Roberts* and Michener's *Tales of the South Pacific* were destined for a stormy courtship followed by an even rockier marriage. The two books were published at about the same time, they dealt with similar themes, they had similar structures and locales, and both were made into highly successful Broadway shows. Michener was not particularly bothered by their parallel paths. Heggen, on the other hand, became tortured by the success of Michener's book, which lead to jealous rages, abusive drinking, and ultimately to self-immolation.

When *Mister Roberts* opened on February 18, 1948, Logan and Heggen along with a cluster of stars were in attendance. Audiences howled at the comedic parts, and afterwards champagne flowed at the first-night parties as the rave reviews came in. Many drama critics called it the best show of the season. The *New York Times*'s Brooks Atkinson ended his column with the line "Thank you, Mr. Heggen and Mr. Logan, for a royal good time."

Tom Heggen, at twenty-eight years of age, was at the zenith of his fame and well on his way to becoming a millionaire. But there was also a nagging downside to his sudden moment in the spotlight. Instead of featuring Heggen's role, many reviews focused on Logan's significant contribution: how he had taken a slender volume of stories and shaped it into a Broadway triumph. Heggen began to grow resentful of both Logan and his part in the production. The morning after opening night, Heggen was scanning the morning papers when he came upon a fresh insult to his already shaken sensibilities. A news story revealed that Joshua Logan's future plans included writing, along with Richard Rodgers and Oscar Hammerstein, a musical based on James A. Michener's *Tales of the South Pacific*. Leland Hayward would produce, and Logan was set to direct the play, which would open sometime next season.

Heggen was aware that Logan was looking into Michener's book for theatrical use, but he had no idea that the director had signed on to write and direct the play. And *Mister Roberts* had just opened! Jealousy and suspicion smoldered inside Heggen. Increasingly he felt "that *South Pacific* was the bastard child of *Mister Roberts*, that the Pacific was *his* ocean and they had snatched it away without so much as a thank you."

Michener met Heggen briefly at a photographic session organized by Time-Life to honor the work of important emerging writers. Their meeting was frosty, to say the least, with only a polite handshake marking their introduction. Three other writers were in attendance: Irwin Shaw, Alfred Hayes, and John Horne Burns. During the session the writers all wore their professional smiles except Heggen, whose expression could be summed up as a demonic scowl.

Michener's *Tales* and the musical *South Pacific* were not the only sources of Heggen's discontent. Throughout the year 1948, worry gnawed at him that he was incapable of following *Mister Roberts* with a second work of equal importance. His descent from Mount Parnassus seemed as sudden as his bold ascent two years before. In May 1949, barely a year and three months after the smash opening of *Mister Roberts* on Broadway, he found himself completely alone. Staying at a friend's apartment, his talent crippled by diffidence, he looked into the future and saw only darkness. He drew himself a bath, got in, lined up some prescription pills near his elbow, and proceeded to let the water, like some soothing Pacific lagoon, bring him peace. The coroner's report was succinct: "Submersion in fresh water in bathtub. Probable suicide. Contributory cause, overdose of barbiturates."

·

The spring of 1948 was one of the most tumultuous periods in Jim's life. *Tales of the South Pacific* was firmly in the capable hands of Rodgers and Hammerstein. As a musical it was now formally known as *South Pacific*. The story collection was earning some spin-off promotion from the association with R&H and was selling well in paperback. Michener was paying regular visits to Carl Brandt's literary agency in hopes of convincing Brandt that he was viable and durable writer. He was also interviewing a young agent named Helen Strauss of the William Morris Agency, who seemed much more willing to take on a fledgling writer than Brandt was.

In addition to placing his new novel *The Fires of Spring* with Brandt, Jim had also shown it to Macmillan, in hopes that *Tales* had been successful enough to win him a second publishing contract. But Macmillan, and especially its president George Brett, balked at extending to Michener another contract. For one thing, Brett wanted Michener as an editor and executive. He did not want Michener to make the disastrous decision to quit Macmillan and pursue the life of a freelance writer. Even more unacceptable to Brett was the possibility that Michener might try to balance continued work at Macmillan with a part-time writing career.

Brett therefore tried to force Michener's hand. One evening in early March he told Michener over dinner in the boardroom that Macmillan was formally rejecting *The Fires of Spring*. Brett disliked it and so had a number of editors, Brett said. Jim was speechless. Switching gears, Brett added smoothly: "Michener, I've been watching you, listening to reports . . . and I'm convinced you have a brilliant future as a publisher. I want you to start immediately working closely with me with an eye to your becoming in due course the president of our company."

Michener was again at a loss. When he collected his senses, he said that he would like to think the offer over. As he rose to leave, Brett remarked: "Michener, you really have no future as a writer but a tremendous one as a publisher."

After some reflection, Michener took his manuscript and headed up to the offices of Random House on Fiftieth Street, where he asked to see the senior editor, Saxe Commins. A reedy, chain-smoking editor much in the mold of Scribner's Maxwell Perkins, Commins was a fixture at Random House and the permanent editor of William Faulkner. Commins was also one of the those old-fashioned editors who pruned writers' manuscripts, lent them money, helped them name their children, and fished them out of bars at three in the morning so they could sober up long enough to finish a book. Michener had met him casually over the last few years and thought he would give Commins, and the premier publisher Random House, a chance to publish his book. Commins promised a speedy decision.

Somewhat relieved, Michener departed on vacation. As the train headed west to Colorado, he weighed his options. The first option was to accept Brett's offer and remain with Macmillan in an executive position, one that would groom him for the presidency of the company. His second option was to stay at Macmillan as an editor and write on the side. This option involved balancing business and art, and Michener knew how often such attempts ended in disaster. His third option was to quit Macmillan and try his hand as a freelance writer. This one was downright traumatic to envision. In the back of his mind, Michener knew that only a slim percentage of writers earned enough to support themselves, let alone make a decent living at the typewriter. But he also knew that his case was different—for he held in his hand the trump card known as *South Pacific* and all the royalties it might eventually generate. Might, eventually: these were the words that bothered him. He also had great hopes for *The Fires of Spring*, even though it was going through a tough acceptance period. All the way to Denver these questions dogged him.

But it was also during these moments of despair and doubt that memories warmed him. He reflected on his years in the South Pacific, which he considered some the sweetest of his life, mainly because danger and tragedy were in the constant embrace of beauty and comedy. Excitement lurked on every new island. He was bound to the navy, and yet he was as free as at any time in his life. He had found a paradise that he knew better than anyone—had even written a book about it. Just tracing his rise as a writer, from his dreary Quonset hut in the steaming jungle to holding in his hand *Tales of the South Pacific*, gave him renewed courage and faith in himself. In many ways he had already fulfilled the Tontouta resolution, which perhaps could guide the decisions that needed to be made in the near future. The faces of the South Pacific, both real and fictional, popped out of nowhere, and he remembered them with deep affection:

the obstreperous Bloody Mary, the vain and proud Aubert Ratard, the gracious admiral Billy Calhoun, the raucous Tony Fry, the devilish Luther Billis, the gaunt but defiant Robert Frisbie, the irrepressible Aggie Grey. The images and sounds of the Pacific war, always persistent, had no order and no end.

In Colorado a few days later, he received a cable from Saxe Commins to the effect that he was "greatly enthusiastic" about the *Fires of Spring* manuscript. Commins even compared Michener to Dickens, a compliment that Michener cherished and hoped was merited: "You have the Dickens feel for people and story. . . . The quality of the manuscript is always exciting, penetrating and compassionate . . . completely honest and so radiant with character." Commins realized that Michener had a great gift for narration, a quality that carried many a Michener novel in the future.

Commins went on to say that the manuscript needed tightening, which could only be accomplished when author and editor were side by side. "I have many ideas on the subject that we can discuss," wrote Commins, "but what is important now is the first glow of enthusiasm for the book itself. It is that, above everything else, which helps to determine the fate of a book in a publishing house." In closing, Commins asked whether Michener preferred a fall or a spring publication date, and whether he wished an advance.

Pleasantly stunned, Michener continued his vacation in the Rockies, returning to New York at the end of March. By then he had resolved to proceed carefully at Macmillan and not make any rash moves. He cordially turned down Brett's offer of a promotion, a decision that Brett graciously accepted. In the meantime, Brett had reconsidered his rejection of *The Fires of Spring*, approaching Michener about it just after his return. Michener, silently glowing with revenge, politely told Brett that Random House had offered a contract and would be publishing in the spring of 1949. Brett, more conciliatory since their last meeting, cautioned him: "I have the strong conviction that unless a lot of work is done on that manuscript before it is published you will be doing yourself a great injustice." They were prophetic words, but at the time Michener was so elated about the prospect of working with Random House that he could not weigh their urgency.

By the end of April, Michener was back at his desk, sifting through textbook manuscripts, playing volleyball at the local YMCA in the evenings, and laying out plans for his next novel. He gloated that he had irons in the fire—two, to be exact, *South Pacific* and *The Fires of Spring*—and now a third was to be added from a most unexpected source.

•

Monday, May 3, unfolded like any day in the work week. The alarm went off at four, and Michener, nursing a glass of cold orange juice, put on some music and stumbled to his writing desk, where he continued work on his next novel. He treasured these hours before his day job, declaring that "the need to write is so pressing for me and the act itself so delectable an experience that with little pause I move eagerly to the next assignment; the ideas are impatient to leap from the prison of my mind." Things proceeded regularly until just before he was to leave for the office, when he received a special delivery envelope from the Brandt Literary Agency. Hastily opening it, he read the contents with shock and dismay. "My agent had reached the regrettable conclusion I had no future as a writer. Therefore he was terminating our contract and would be returning my manuscript under separate cover, for he doubted it would ever be publishable." Driving home the blow, Brandt said that Michener "showed no promise of developing into a writer whose works would find favor with the public . . . and that consequently I had no place in his stable."

Although the words cut deep, Michener shaved and dressed for work. At the office, his boss Phil Knowlton first badgered him about some correspondence that Michener had mishandled and then lectured Jim on his abuse of the English language. "Michener," roared Knowlton, "I've told you a score of times, the word *data* is plural. *Data are insufficient. Data do not support.*" As the day wore on, the conversation became more genial. Michener was still with Knowlton when Cecil Scott burst in and exclaimed:

"Jim, you've won the Pulitzer Prize!"

Within minutes colleagues swarmed around, cheering Michener and his triumph. The shell-shocked author did his best to accept congratulations and sort through his feelings. For one thing, he did not know that *Tales of the South Pacific* was even in the running. He expected at any minute a phone call retracting the announcement. Scott, however, was emphatic: *Tales* had won the most coveted and prestigious award in American letters for works published in 1947. "It was both exhilarating and tremendously bewildering," recalled Michener; "in those first few moments I had no conception of either what it meant then or what it would mean in the future."

The phone started ringing, asking Michener for interviews. Late that afternoon—after being fired by his agent, excoriated by his boss, and awarded the Pulitzer Prize, all in the same day—Michener headed down to the studios of WOR Radio for his first-ever literary interview.

"Why do you suppose the Pulitzer committee chose your unusual book?" the reporter at the station asked.

"I really don't know," a dazed Michener replied. "It's sort of miraculous."

The Prize

The winning of the Pulitzer Prize for fiction brought Michener immediate adulation and equal amounts of criticism. During the awards ceremony, he shared the limelight with other notable recipients including Tennessee Williams for drama (*A Streetcar Named Desire*), W. H. Auden for poetry (*The Age of Anxiety*), and Bernard DeVoto for history (*Across the Wide Missouri*). A $1,000 check accompanied the award, and Michener characteristically deposited it in his savings account. Pocket Books immediately increased its press run of the paperback edition of *Tales* to 250,000. Fans and well-wishers deluged him with mail. Rodgers and Hammerstein telegrammed their kudos from Los Angeles: "Congratulations and salutes to you and hooray for our judgment exclamation point." Henceforth, the phrase "from the Pulitzer Prize winning novel by James A. Michener" would always appear in official credits for *South Pacific*.

But some members of the press were outraged over the selection. Writing in the Sunday *World Herald*, Victor Haas summed up the sentiment among many critics: "Mr. Michener's 'novel' is, in reality, a collection of 19 stories. . . . Don't misunderstand me—Mr. Michener has written some good short stories, but I do not find them 'distinguished.'"

Years after the Pulitzer Prize announcement, reviewers were still debating the selection of Michener's book. Writing in the mid-1960's in *Pulitzer Prize Novels: A Critical Backward Look*, W. J. Stuckey asserted: "Only by a liberal stretch of one's definition can *Tales of the South Pacific* be called distinguished fiction. It is simply a collection of descriptions, character sketches, unconnected incidents, anecdotes, off-color jokes, patriotic editorials, all loosely held together by a central narrator who can see into the minds of other people and report what is happening in places miles away. . . . The examples of bad writing are almost inexhaustible."

The focus of critical attention appeared to be on whether the definition of "novel" could include a collection of stories, and whether *Tales* rose to the level of "distinguished fiction." A lesser consideration, though still important, was whether it portrayed "American life," as stipulated in the language accompanying the award.

Since the first awards in 1917, the Pulitzer Prizes have been bestowed on some of the great luminaries in American fiction, including Booth Tarkington, Sinclair Lewis, Willa Cather, Thornton Wilder, Margaret Mitchell, John Steinbeck, and Robert Penn Warren. The prizes have also undergone subtle and sometimes drastic shifts dictated by changing tastes and trends. Originally the judges were instructed to scrutinize works for their patriotism and sound morals. The novel prize was to be awarded annually "for the American novel published during the year which shall best present the wholesome atmosphere of American life and the highest standard of American manners and manhood." From the beginning, however, there were problems with the official language, and by 1929 the wording had been changed to "For the best American novel published during the year, preferably one which shall best present the whole atmosphere of American life." This language further complicated matters, as both jurors and the Advisory Board, who have the final say on the prize, debated what defined an "American novel" and what was meant by "the whole atmosphere of American life." What did the "whole" mean? Did the official language mean that to win the award an author had to squeeze the whole of American life into one novel? And did the "whole" encompass both the wholesome and unwholesome characteristics of American life? Such ambiguities led to further refining of the citation. By 1934 the wording ran: "for the best novel published during the year by an American author, preferably dealing with American life."

Even this language caused problems. Responsible for scanning hundreds of novels and reducing their final list to five, the jurors—generally three in any given year, sometimes just two—suggested it would be easier, and certainly less stressful, to proclaim a book meritorious without having to assert it was the "best" of the lot. Hence the word "best" was dropped in favor of "distinguished."

Beginning in 1934, jurors were instructed not to recommend one novel for the award, but rather to nominate several candidates along with their reasons for submitting them. The final decision rested with the Advisory Board, which was made up of newspaper publishers and editors. Jurors were usually writers and critics, serving for three to five years. For the 1948 award, three top-notch jurors recommended the final titles: John Chamberlain of *Time* magazine, Maxwell Geismar, writer and critic, and Orville Prescott of the *New York Times*, the reviewer who had raved about *Tales of the South Pacific*.

On May 10, 1947, a full year before Michener was awarded the Pulitzer Prize, the accompanying language was again revised. In order to accommodate shorter works of fiction, the Pulitzer committee changed the wording for the novel to "distinguished fiction in book form, preferably dealing with American life." This change widened the scope of the Pulitzer Prize and opened the door for short story collections—which many people asserted included *Tales of the South Pacific*. But what was meant by "American life"? Did it only include events occurring within the borders of the United States? Or could it also include the experiences of Americans abroad, such as in China or France or the Solomons? There was precedent for broad interpretation of this phrase. In 1944, for example, the Pulitzer was awarded to John Hersey for *A Bell for Adano*, which depicted American GIs in Italy during the war. Military units operating in foreign countries, therefore, became prime candidates for consideration.

In the decision-making process for the 1948 Pulitzer Prize for fiction, conducted in absolute secrecy, the jurors eliminated more than three hundred novels published in 1947 and focused on five: A. B. Guthrie's *The Big Sky*, Willard Motley's *Knock on Any Door*, Saul Bellow's *The Stoic*, Gerald Warner Brace's *The Garretson Chronicle*, and Michener's *Tales*. Each juror had his favorite. Chamberlain favored *Knock on Any Door*; Geismar liked *The Big Sky* and *The Stoic*; Prescott pressed for *Tales of the South Pacific*. When the time came to submit their final recommendations, they sent, unranked, their five finalists to the Advisory Board.

Because no title was a consensus choice for that year, the Advisory Board considered giving no award, as was the case in 1920 and again in 1941. For many days in April 1948 the Advisory Board deliberated, with no front-runner emerging. The chairman of the board was veteran newsman Arthur Krock, Washington bureau chief for the *New York Times*. In late April Krock received a telephone call from Alice Roosevelt Longworth, eldest daughter of Theodore Roosevelt and widow of Speaker of the House of Representatives Nicholas Longworth. Coltish, fiercely outspoken, and frequently improper, Alice Longworth was a doyenne of Washington society. She also wielded tremendous influence. In their conversation, Krock let slip one of book titles that had a good chance of winning the Pulitzer for fiction. "That's a nothing work! No vitality!" cried Longworth. And she then suggested to Krock that the only book fit for this year's award was *Tales of the South Pacific*, whose ribald scenes and exotic locales had won her over. Evidently Krock was mightily persuaded, for he immediately reread the book, called the Advisory Board together, and steered its decision. "I gave my reasons for selecting *Tales*," said Krock, "and the Board accepted them."

The Pulitzer controversy rattled Michener's normally sound confidence. He singled out other works that merited the award, most notably John Horne Burns's story cycle *The Gallery*. Published in the summer of 1947, *The Gallery* was a penetrating study of American soldiers in the Mediterranean theater, notably in the Galleria Umberto I in Naples. "I liked the book," remarked Michener, "because of its daring subject matter, finding it an American equivalent of E. M. Forster and André Gide." Admittedly gay, Burns became the outcast member of the Pulitzer field for 1948. When the Pulitzer Prize was announced, Burns conceived "a blazing hatred" for Michener, "feeling with justification" that Jim "had robbed him of a prize that was rightfully his." For many months thereafter, Michener continued to sing the praises of Burns's book—in Jim's mind the rightful winner of the 1948 Pulitzer Prize for fiction.

Michener also reasoned that *Tales* could have won only in that particular year, when the Pulitzer field seemed thin. He cited the previous year, when Robert Penn Warren's *All The King's Men* stood virtually without peer in the competition and went on to become an American classic. The Pulitzer for 1949 went to James Gould Cozzens's *Guard of Honor*, another novel Michener felt would have crushed *Tales* head to head. So luck, timing, and the lack of a serious rival, Michener believed, had vaulted *Tales* into the national spotlight.

Despite the flap over the book's eminence, Michener still thought that he faithfully captured American and Melanesian life as it unfolded during the war in the Pacific. Doubt, however, lingered. "There was a flurry of interest in me following the Pulitzer Prize and a lot of invitations resulted, but I didn't have the skill to fill them. As a result I wasted a lot of time and heartache. I've *never* had that confidence many [writers] seem to possess. I have a sense of competence—I'm a competent workman—but maybe it's best one doesn't have that confidence; makes you cautious; keeps you from making a damn fool of yourself."

In the late spring and summer of 1948, two important women dominated Jim's life. The first was the buoyant and savvy literary agent Helen Strauss of the William Morris Agency, whom Jim had selected to be his agent. Strauss recognized that Michener was a man of considerable complexity. He was a loner, but he took direction willingly and he was probably the hardest-working writer she had seen in her three years at the agency. His greatest quirk, however, was his ability to isolate himself in a crowd. Once, in the middle of a social gathering, Jim reached in his pocket, made some notes on pad, then got up and went into the next room to continue some writing he was working on, leaving other guests puzzled as to his whereabouts.

For the next twenty years, until she left New York for Hollywood, Michener and Strauss orchestrated one of the great author-agent relationships in publishing, in the process turning out blockbuster novels, movie deals, spin-off journal articles, and foreign translations. His association with Random House, which lasted nearly fifty years, was similarly cordial and productive, producing enduring friendships with fellow writers such as Truman Capote and Gore Vidal and Random publishing executives Bennett Cerf and Donald Klopfer.

The other woman in Jim's life was Vange Nord, a twenty-five-year-old architecture student he met at a party. After several intense months of courtship, he flew to Reno for a speedy divorce from his first wife. Sophisticated and given to name-dropping, Vange was the opposite of Patti Koon Michener. Through Jim she hoped to advance her own writing career, which was barely in the fledgling stage. When they married in the summer of 1948, she was freelancing for several magazines and beginning to develop plans for her first novel.

Although Michener felt wounded by the literary world's assessment of his first book, he limped ahead knowing that Random House was polishing his second work for next spring's launch and that near Doylestown Oscar Hammerstein was developing *South Pacific* into a Broadway musical. With his new wife, and with his old job at Macmillan anchoring his financial life, he had every reason to be optimistic.

Mary and Ezio

Between the farm near Doylestown and his spacious Manhattan office, Oscar Hammerstein toiled on the book and lyrics of *South Pacific*. For many readers *Tales* was a picaresque adventure of rogues and war heroes; for Hammerstein the adventure was in finding a narrative center on which to build a hit musical. Without a protagonist or a strong story line, *Tales* appeared to defy dramatization. Oscar pored over Michener's stories, heavily marking certain sections and focusing on material that would translate well to the stage. After a month of labor, he presented to Rodgers an outline that framed two chapters, "Fo' Dolla'" and "Our Heroine." He liked the interplay of characters in the former, particularly the banter between Bloody Mary and Lieutenant Cable, and Cable's intense but doomed relationship with Liat. In "Our Heroine" he liked the unforced nobility of Emile and the puckish innocence of Nellie. He was also drawn to Bali Ha'i as a central symbol that could be used as a backdrop to the players and the action.

Concerns mounted, however, as Oscar built the show in his mind. One was that the Cable-Liat relationship might parallel *Madama Butterfly* too much, so he reconsidered all the stories before finally settling on "Fo' Dolla'" as one of the primary segments in the show. The rakish Tony Fry appealed to Oscar, and he originally wrote him into the show as a central figure. But Fry's character was eventually eclipsed by that of Luther Billis, who provided the necessary comic relief from the two central romantic stories. Another consideration was to make the show part ballet, but this was rejected on the grounds that *Tales* was foremost a serious and realistic view of war.

Hammerstein realized that the central theme was prejudice, the same feature that ignited Michener's book. The challenge was to bring the two stories together and have them move toward some dramatic climax. Oscar solved this by introducing Operation Alligator at the beginning of the show and having it collect the characters in its sweep. All characters would then be driven by the military operation and eventually be affected by it.

In musical theater at the time, if two love stories were introduced, the primary love story should be serious while the secondary one should be comic and lighthearted. Hammerstein, and later Joshua Logan, decided to break with theater tradition and use the two serious love stories, providing comic relief with the madcap antics of Luther Billis. It was a bold gamble on Oscar's part, but he was by now more willing than ever to take risks.

Because *South Pacific* is heavily romantic, most people assumed that only two of Michener's stories were used on the stage. Aiding this misconception was the fact that the Emile-Nellie love story was left out of the original paperback edition because of space considerations. People therefore assumed it was a creation of Rodgers and Hammerstein. Looking for all types of visual and dramatic background features, Oscar plundered virtually every one of Michener's tales. The shower built out from a tree in "Dry Rot" became a set for Nellie's hair-washing scene. The Professor, a minor character in "The Airstrip at Konora," became Luther Billis's companion. Ngana and Jerome, the names of Emile's children in the stage version, were borrowed from two of the Remittance Man's comrades in "The Cave." The Remittance Man's story inspired Oscar to take another bold step. Instead of using a disembodied radio voice, he made Emile de Becque the brave man who travels into enemy territory to transmit Japanese naval movements. His daring mission gives Emile a way of redeeming himself in Nellie's eyes, and also brings together the Frenchman and Cable for the pivotal climax of the musical. Oscar wanted the mission to transform Emile from a passive member of the Free French into a hero capable of winning Nellie's heart.

Things were going well with the show, albeit not perfectly. Hammerstein still had not worked out many of the issues dealing with the libretto and the staging of the scenes. Rodgers had barely started on the music. After two months most of *South Pacific* was still very much in limbo. In mid-May, while Michener dealt with the news of the Pulitzer Prize, Rodgers and Hammerstein received a telephone call from Edwin Lester, the Los Angeles Civic Light Opera Association's producer. Lester reported that he had signed Ezio Pinza, the esteemed Metropolitan Opera basso, to a $25,000 contract to star in his next production, which unfortunately was closing before it even opened. Lester wondered if R&H could use Pinza and take over his salary.

Hammerstein listened intently, for he had begun to flirt with the idea of making Emile de Becque the lead character, relegating the Liat-Cable story to a secondary role. Emile was in his forties, already older than most leading men in the theater. Pinza had just turned fifty-six, so it was a further risk to cast him in the role.

Ezio Pinza initially trained to be a professional cyclist in his native Italy, but left to pursue opera. He debuted in 1919 at the age of twenty-seven, and seven years later he gave his first New York performance. Appearing more than eight hundred times, Pinza became one of the enduring stars of the Met. In such difficult roles as Boris Godunov and Don Giovanni, he thrilled audiences throughout the 1930s and early 1940s. After the war, however, Pinza reached a turning point in his career. "I had become restless, having exhausted the repertoire available for my voice and sung in every major opera house and concert house in the world. . . . I was looking for new fields to conquer."

At the Bel Air Hotel in Los Angeles, Rodgers and Hammerstein met Pinza, who was now eager for theater roles. Hammerstein lent him a copy of *Tales of the South Pacific*. Pinza felt an immediate identification with the French planter. "He was a kindred soul into whose shoes I stepped with the greatest ease," Pinza observed. "We were both Latins of about the same age, both of whom fell in love with a much younger American girl. In each case, the man had to fight in order to get her, and fight he did. I also sympathized with Emile's enlightened views on problems of race and color." Big-boned and moving with a lumbering grace, Pinza also mirrored many of Emile's physical qualities.

By the time Rodgers and Hammerstein arrived back in New York, the two were virtually sold on the Italian basso. But Rodgers first had to hear him sing in person. In June Pinza performed before a Manhattan radio audience; Dick and Oscar were in the audience, and were wowed by Pinza's voice and range. A contract soon followed, stipulating that Pinza did not have to sing more than fifteen minutes of material in any performance. Rodgers and Hammerstein budged a good deal more with Pinza than with any previous star, but then again, no one of the Italian's stature had ever been involved with an R&H production before.

Rodgers and Hammerstein had gone fishing and landed the "big one." Almost overnight, after the signing of Pinza, the Emile-Nellie relationship had taken precedence in the show. Now the team had to find a Nellie capable of matching Pinza's charisma and talent. "As long as we've got Pinza," Hammerstein remarked, "let's go the whole hog. Let's get Mary Martin to play Nellie." For Rodgers, who worshipped her, Martin made complete sense for the role. They needed someone fresh, sprightly, and preferably Southern, as Nellie was from Arkansas. Martin was from Texas, directly across the border. Even in shades of her talking and singing voice, Martin had to sound like Nellie. For a solid hour Rodgers and Hammerstein hashed over the pros and cons of casting Martin. When the session ended, they had their number one—and sole—choice. It remained only to persuade Martin to accept the role.

Martin was currently starring in the road show of *Annie Get Your Gun* in California. Oscar and Dick called her and asked if she would like to appear next to Pinza. At the time, she was performing Ethel Merman's songs eight times a week, causing her soprano voice to be lowered nearly a full octave. Her voice crackled on the long distance line: "What on earth do you want, two basses?" She was terrified of playing next to Pinza, whose soaring operatic voice might waft her into the next theater. Rodgers assured her she would never appear in competition with the Italian basso. They would sing in turn, not together. She promised Rodgers they would talk further after she and her husband-manager Richard Halliday returned to the East Coast later that summer.

Back in New York, Martin went to a Pinza recital and became further convinced that he was on a level by himself. Rodgers invited the Hallidays to his Connecticut home to hear some of the show's songs. At this time, Hammerstein had written only the first scene with Nellie and Emile and a comprehensive outline. Oscar Hammerstein and Joshua Logan were also in attendance, walking Martin through many of the opening scenes. With Rodgers at the piano and Hammerstein voicing the lyrics, they played "A Cockeyed Optimist," "Twin Soliloquies," and "Some Enchanted Evening." "Oh, the impact of that song!" Martin recalled. After a memorable afternoon, she promised to get back to the team within seventy-two hours.

That night, she remembered, "Richard and I talked about the glorious song 'Some Enchanted Evening.' We were both sure that no matter whether the show was a success or not, that would be one of the memorable songs of the musical stage. It wasn't 'mine,' it was Ezio's. But that didn't matter." At three o'clock in the morning, Mary picked up the phone and dialed Rodgers. "Do I have to wait three days? Can't I say yes right now?"

With two major talents under contract, the next step was putting their egos in check. Martin and Pinza eventually agreed that they would be paid the same amount, and that neither would get top billing: their names would appear side by side on the program and on the marquee. As production went into full swing, they both consented to making the show, not their individual parts, the primary focus. Pinza, unlike the veteran Martin, found the musical stage a bumpy adjustment. "It was the first time I had been in a purely American show," Pinza explained, "the language of which was almost as far removed from the English used in opera as from a foreign tongue. I had expected that I would have to make certain readjustments, but it had never occurred to me that they might be so difficult."

.

After several more casting decisions, Hammerstein called Michener in Doylestown to update him on the progress of *South Pacific*. Jim was elated to hear that Pinza had won the role of Emile. For many years opera had been in Michener's blood. He remembered the time in his childhood when his uncle Arthur lugged a Victrola into the house and they first played a record featuring Enrico Caruso. Mary Martin was also well known to Jim, and the pairing could not have pleased him more. Oscar also said they had cast the versatile Juanita Hall as Bloody Mary and Betta St. John as Liat. He, Rodgers, and Logan were still in the midst of casting Lieutenant Cable and several other roles.

In the meantime, Jim had received the galley proofs for *The Fires of Spring* from Saxe Commins, and he was busy correcting them. His second book would present him with one of his most difficult periods as an author. Expectations following his Pulitzer Prize–winning *Tales* were astronomical. While the public turned *The Fires of Spring* into a best seller, the critics did everything to undermine it. Calling it "sententious," "corny," and "sentimental," critics from New York to Los Angeles pummeled the novel.

Michener prepared himself as best he could for the criticism. He decided very early in his career that he would always keep a level head, no matter whether the reviews were adverse or extremely positive. What the critics saw was a new side of Michener's art, one that would reappear in the years ahead. Michener knew that one of his great weaknesses was trying to be operatic with his dramatic scenes, of announcing them with the force of an atomic organ. "I have been damaged, in some ways," he wrote, "by my fixation on opera, for it has helped to delude me into seeing human experience in a more dramatic form . . . and it has encouraged me toward artistic conventions that I might have done well to avoid." While Michener in his second book may have been trying to be clever and literary, critics saw artifice and insincerity.

One of the most devastating reviews came from John Horne Burns, who took the opportunity to avenge his loss of the Pulitzer to Michener. Writing in the *Saturday Review*, Burns declared, among other things, that *The Fires of Spring* was "brilliant high school stuff" full of "soggy prose" and "embarrassing dialogue." The *Saturday Review* and its editor Norman Cousins had even made plans to run Michener's picture on the cover, but after Burns's vitriolic criticism the magazine had to cancel it.

Burns of course had given Michener an invitation to hate him back. However, just the opposite happened. As the months went on, Michener began to see Burns more as an ally than as the enemy. Michener even praised Burns's second novel when all others were scorning it. As he had with Tom Heggen, Michener bonded to his abuser, and he followed Burns's short career with interest. He saw Burns as his alter ego, perhaps to the point of considering Burns a better writer than himself. When Burns died of a cerebral hemorrhage in Italy at the age of thirty-six, Michener was deeply saddened. "I began to appreciate the great loss I had suffered," Michener wrote, "for men often thrive when they have competitors against whom to test themselves, and had Burns lived I am sure he and I would have competed, honorably and vigorously, throughout our lives, each checking what the other was doing . . . each going his unique way, each presenting a mirror-image of the other."

Josh and Oscar

After a brief vacation, a reenergized Joshua Logan returned to the *South Pacific* project and found that things were not proceeding well. He had expected the libretto to be finished, but Oscar had gotten bogged down. Oscar always preferred writing lyrics to writing the book. Lyrics were much easier and did not present the endless complications of writing dialogue and developing plot points. One morning on the phone Oscar admitted to Josh that he had hit a wall. "I know absolutely nothing about Army behavior or how a sergeant talks to a general, and vice versa," he said. "I hate the military so much that I'm ignorant of it." Since most of *South Pacific* is steeped in military practice, Josh sensed that Oscar—and the whole show—was in bad straits.

Logan, who knew his Code of Conduct and chain of command by heart, told Oscar he would drive down to Doylestown and they could work out the difficulties together. "Oh, please do, Josh. Dorothy would love for you and Nedda to stay here. Come down this afternoon. I need you."

In addition to his brilliance as a director, one of Logan's most endearing characteristics to his friends and family was his altruism. Without thinking, he would step in and help anyone in peril, much to the dismay of his wife. Nedda loved Josh for this quality but often thought that people took advantage of him.

As they drove down to Doylestown, she reflected that in helping out Oscar, Josh might be exceeding his role as a director, a concern that on this occasion she did not mention to her husband. The Logans did not plan to stay any length of time, just long enough for Josh to break the logjam involving Oscar and the libretto. This hope, however, proved vain.

It took Josh only a few hours of reviewing the script with Hammerstein to realize the scope of the issue. Although the main stories and the lead performers had been chosen, much of the continuity of the book and some of the songs were yet to be written. A major difficulty was Oscar's lack of military knowledge. "What do sailors do when young Lieutenant Cable comes onto the beach?" he asked Josh. "I had them snapping to attention. But that seemed wrong."

"Good God, yes," answered Logan. "They'd pretend he wasn't there."

When they cleared up some of these details, the book started gaining momentum. The Logans' sojourn at Highland Farm turned from overnight into several days. Using a Dictaphone, Oscar and Josh role-played the scene when Bloody Mary first makes her appearance. "I was Billis, I was a Seabee, I was Lieutenant Cable," Josh recalled. "For me, military dialogue flowed easily. Oscar was amazed. When I got to Bloody Mary, suddenly he was talking and I was repeating his words into the mouthpiece. We . . . kept on dictating into the night and through the next day. There was no more talk of my going back to New York. I just stayed." .

For the next week the Hammerstein living room was transformed into a virtual theater. As Josh brainstormed through the outline, Oscar developed a substantial portion of the book. With Josh often dancing and gesturing wildly and Oscar prompting him with bits of business, many of the ensemble scenes involving Bloody Mary and the Seabees were developed. The two men's secretaries typed up the proceedings, while the wives collated the pages on the floor.

Long walks around Highland Farm also stimulated their creativity. This was the countryside that inspired Oscar's "Oh, What a Beautiful Mornin'" from *Oklahoma!* and many pastoral lyrics from *Carousel*. They talked and joked in the shade of large elms and maples, or leaned back on one of the fence rails and mused, then raced back to the house to write down their ideas, scattering a flock of geese and ducks waddling up the lawn.

As Josh worked feverishly during the day and collapsed into bed each night, Nedda raised her concerns. "You're writing again and you only signed a contract to direct," she told him. "Oscar was to write it by himself."

"I know, but crazy as it may sound, he *can't* write this one. He doesn't understand the military or Little Rock."

"Then you must tell him in the morning that you can't continue unless you're his *collaborator*."

Suddenly, Josh felt cornered. He told Nedda that he didn't think Oscar wanted a collaborator.

"Who cares," she said, "he's *got* a collaborator—one *he asked for.* You don't like giving away your ideas any more than he does, do you? He's a grown man and a businessman, and so are you. Tell him tomorrow."

Everything Nedda said was true. Oscar had asked Josh to help him, but Logan could not bring himself to provoke a showdown in the midst of this hectic birthing process. He delayed telling Hammerstein until months later, when it was nearly too late.

After some two weeks of exhausting and exhilarating work, the Logans returned to New York, leaving Oscar to polish the remainder of libretto and his final lyrics for *South Pacific.* Josh left knowing he was about to direct the most important show of his career. It is difficult to assess just how much of the final book Josh Logan was responsible for. Some estimates say 30 to 40 percent. But the percentage was not as critical perhaps as his knowledge of military lore and directing for the theater, without which the creation of *South Pacific* would have collapsed during that summer of 1948.

•

By early autumn preproduction was on a roll. Hammerstein kept Michener apprised of script changes and additions to the cast. He also asked him to write some notes about what Luther Billis might do in his spare time, for use as away-from-the-action visuals. Jim remained in awe of the process as it gained momentum, and Oscar frequently invited him to Josh's apartment where he could hear the debut of his latest lyrics accompanied by Rodgers's music. When asked by the newspapers how he liked the translation of his book to the stage, Jim gleefully replied: "I can only say they have accomplished a remarkable feat of juggling without ever mussing an eyebrow of one of the characters."

More than most productions of the same scope, *South Pacific* represented a grand feat of collaboration to come up with some of the most glorious music, suspenseful plot turns, and captivating stage effects.

From the very beginning, Oscar wanted to make Bali Ha'i the central emotional symbol of the musical. When he wrote the first two lines of the song, "Most people live on a lonely island / Lost in the middle of a foggy sea," he created the notion that we are essentially lonely creatures seeking connection with others. Josh and Oscar worked on ways to integrate the island's presence with the human activity on the naval base. When they were writing the segment where Cable is left alone on the beach, suddenly the two shouted together, "The island calls him!" From that point on, Oscar could finish the lyrics and have Bali Ha'i "call" the Seabees to its romantic shores. The personification of the island worked: Bali Ha'i became as much a vibrant character as Bloody Mary or Nellie Forbush.

When Oscar's lyrics were finished, the team along with Michener gathered at the Logans' apartment. Dick Rodgers read Oscar's words, turned the paper over and scribbled some notes, then got up and went to the piano. Five minutes later he had the finished score for "Bali Ha'i." Rodgers explained: "I knew the melody would have to possess an Oriental, languorous quality, that it would have to be suitable for contralto voice. . . . Therefore, as soon as I read the words I could hear the music to go with them. If you know your trade, the actual writing should never take long."

A few days later, set designer Jo Mielziner began the task of creating the scenic backdrop that would forcefully convey Rodgers's music and Hammerstein's lyrics. His first watercolor sketch featured the serrated volcanic shape of the island across the greenish water. Sensing that it needed more mystery, he soaked his brush in water and blurred the faint top of the island so that it appeared enveloped in mist. Rodgers and Hammerstein saw its possibilities very quickly.

This iconic image of Bali Ha'i, created by Michener, expanded upon by Logan and Hammerstein and Rodgers, depicted by Mielziner, and copied by many, survived the decades and became the enduring symbol of man's vision of an exotic, and often unreachable, paradise.

•

Three months before the show's opening night, Josh Logan still had not secured credit for the book. Nedda prodded him constantly, but neither Hammerstein nor Rodgers said a word about it. He spent sleepless nights telling himself, "It's going to win the Pulitzer Prize, and no one will ever know I wrote a word of it."

When the simmer turned to a boil, he mustered his courage and approached Oscar, who was visiting the Logans. Oscar was reading the last pages of the libretto when Josh walked in. "You look strange," said Oscar.

"I'm fine, fine," Josh stammered, trying to get the words out. "Oscar, I think I should get half credit for the book."

For a moment Hammerstein reflected, blushing slightly. "Of course you must have credit. After all, you wrote it as much as I did. We'll work out the exact credits later."

Logan's relief, however, was only temporary. The next afternoon Oscar, looking "painfully stern," told Logan that things had changed. He had conferred with Rodgers and his lawyers, and Josh would indeed get the credit he wanted—coauthorship of the libretto. But there were strings attached, said Oscar. "According to our contract, in the credits your name as director was to be in the same type size as mine and Dick's. But now Dick and I must have the top one hundred percent credit with the lead-in 'A Musical Play By Rodgers and Hammerstein.'" Oscar explained that his and Logan's names, as coauthors of the book, would appear below in smaller type (60 percent). Worse, Logan's director's credit would be reduced to 60 percent as well. And the carnage was not over.

"It goes without saying," said Oscar, "that you won't get anything whatsoever of the author's royalties."

This was the ultimate blow for Logan. A director's royalties ended when the individual production ceased, but an author's royalties continued forever and included foreign rights, film rights, and licensing of amateur shows. After catching his breath, Josh pleaded with Oscar to reconsider.

"Josh," said Oscar painfully. "Rodgers and Hammerstein cannot and *will not* share a copyright. It's part of their financial structure. Including you would weaken our position. . . . It's impossible."

In a last-second bid to salvage what remained of his honor and also to secure future royalties, Josh asked Hammerstein if he could transfer a part of his director's share to a coauthor's share. "It wouldn't cost the show any more," reasoned Logan, "and then I would at least have some of the future earnings."

Oscar said that his lawyers would consider it, but he later reiterated that it was not a possibility. Logan, who wanted to be part of *South Pacific* more than anything else, was left with these results: he would direct *South Pacific* as contracted and receive royalties as long as the show continued; he would receive credit for coauthorship of the book, but his name would be in smaller print as both coauthor and director; and he would receive no author's royalties for his efforts.

Joshua Logan had run up against one of the most formidable partnerships in show business, and lost. By the late 1940s Rodgers and Hammerstein wielded as much power in the entertainment world as movie companies such as MGM or Twentieth Century Fox. Rodgers and the R&H lawyers were acute businessmen. Many who knew them assumed that Rodgers directed business matters and Hammerstein went along with his decisions. But Oscar, although he preferred to work on the creative aspects of a musical, was always privy to business matters. And he was no pushover in the matter of giving credit where it was deserved. "He could have mowed Dick down if he had wanted to," observed Logan. Despite his tender qualities, his sympathetic understanding of the underdog, his optimistic belief in a better world, Hammerstein was as driven by self-interest as any creative person. When it came to Josh Logan's case, he bought into the idea, submitted by the lawyers and agreed upon by Rodgers, that no one, not even a friend, could infringe upon the inviolable names of Rodgers and Hammerstein.

The day after his critical discussions with Oscar, Logan left for Bill Brown's Health Farm, where he frequently went to rest and recuperate before starting rehearsals. While he was there, Rodgers and Hammerstein's lawyer Howard Reinheimer sent Logan's lawyer a contract, with the stipulation that if it was not signed within two hours, then Logan need not come to rehearsals. In other words, R&H would hire another director. Logan's lawyer signed.

Recoiling from this mistreatment, Josh threw himself into the rehearsals. He dealt with his disappointment by reminding himself of his warm feelings for Hammerstein. Although he respected and revered Rodgers, he had a strong connection to Hammerstein. He had worked with Rodgers for more than ten years and they had developed a very positive working relationship. But all this seemed to evaporate quickly. He now described Rodgers as "a brilliant, talented, highly intelligent, theatrically sound superbrain" who had been diminished by his own "stratospheric fame."

For many days after the contract issue, Logan's heart was as heavy as an anchor. However, he was also a consummate professional, and as time went on, as he became swept up in Rodgers's music and the performers' excitement, he was once again a confident and assured stage director.

•

It was a widely accepted principle that social commentary—particularly involving issues of race and discrimination—had no place in the American musical theater. Hammerstein did not set out to write a play with a strong protest element, but Michener's tales, which revolved around themes of prejudice and intolerance, forced him to consider these themes in his lyrics. For one thing, he needed a song to capture the emotion of Lieutenant Cable when he abandons Liat. In writing the song "You've Got to Be Carefully Taught," he suggested that prejudice was not innate, that it was systematically conveyed from parents to their children. In 1949 such talk was not only controversial, it was downright inflammatory. The postwar world remained a place where ill feeling and resentment toward Japanese and by extension all Asians still lingered.

For many months the song teetered on the brink of being cut. Rodgers, Hammerstein, and Logan liked it. But many who saw the rehearsals urged the team to remove it before opening night, for they could see the whole show being sabotaged by one foolish—albeit noble—mistake. Hammerstein called Michener and asked him if the song should remain. Michener was at first cautious. Having the racial issue in his book was one thing, but having it presented onstage to a variety of audiences was quite another. In the end, Michener insisted that the song stay in the production: "I realize very well the dangers of overstating the case. But I just feel the case is not fully stated without this song. I wish it were true that all these things were accepted by the public."

Like Michener, Hammerstein had an aroused sense of justice and social equality. When an interviewer asked him about his reported love for people, he replied: "I don't idealize people. I am conscious of their imperfections. In fact, I haven't got a high opinion of human beings. . . . I don't think everyone is beautiful or wonderful. . . . I know damned well they are not." The alternative to hate, he remarked, was not blind love but tolerance and understanding. When the interview suggested that understanding might be a path to love, Hammerstein bristled and said, "Not necessarily. I understand a lot of people I don't like at all."

"You've Got to Be Carefully Taught" helped cement the relationship between Michener and Hammerstein, the unusually strident lyrics capturing their mutual sentiments on race relations. However, it was not just in the theater that Oscar and Jim demonstrated their social activism. In the same year that *South Pacific* debuted, Nobel Prize winner and fellow Bucks County resident Pearl Buck founded Welcome House, an adoption agency that placed Asian and Asian-American children in loving homes. Many of the children were abandoned overseas by American servicemen. When traditional agencies refused to take the children, Buck stepped in and started her own adoption agency. Placing these children was a tough process, as discrimination against "half-breeds" and "hybrids" remained strong.

Michener and Hammerstein became two of the staunchest supporters of Welcome House. Eventually Oscar acquired two grandchildren through the agency. Similarly, Michener and his wife Vange adopted two Asian-American children through Welcome House.

Clearly, Michener and Hammerstein were committed to improving postwar race relations in both their public and their private lives. Only time would tell whether such a commitment would jeopardize the success of *South Pacific*.

CHAPTER 13

Those Enchanted Evenings

On March 7, exactly a month away from its Broadway premiere, *South Pacific* opened for a trial run at the Shubert Theater in New Haven, Connecticut. It arrived in New England in sound financial shape. The four producers were able to finance the musical, not by the usual limited partnership, but by forming a corporation with a maximum of ten investors. The producers raised a total of $225,000, but because *South Pacific* cost only $180,000 they were in a position to return the remainder to stockholders on the day the musical debuted on Broadway.

As he sat watching the world premiere with his wife, James Michener enjoyed the best of both worlds. He relished the role of original author of the musical and all the attention that went with it; he also enjoyed sitting back and watching the professionals do their work. During the performance, he was so moved that he had to go out to the lobby and compose himself before rejoining Vange. He had seen several rehearsals, but the full force of the music and the performers in this pre-Broadway tryout hit him in successive waves. On these few occasions he bumped into Hammerstein and Rodgers, who were posted like sentinels at the rear doors hoping to gauge the crowd's reaction to each scene and musical number. The crowd did react. They applauded after every number, lengthening the show but giving Rodgers the clear sense they loved the music.

The New Haven tryout became crucial in identifying both strengths and weaknesses in the show, and affording enough time to correct the latter before it moved onto the boards of the Majestic Theatre in New York. The strengths clearly were the book, lyrics, music, and talented lead performers. However, while singing "A Wonderful Guy" in rehearsals, Mary Martin had once cartwheeled into the orchestra pit and flattened the pianist, Trude Rittman. "Mary had landed on Trude's shoulders, breaking her own fall but knocking Trude out. Trude came to quickly, severely shaken and in pain," according to Josh Logan. "We had been within inches of terminal disaster. Instead of a cartwheel we substituted a good, safe high note."

Martin had gotten a short, gamine haircut just before rehearsals. Surprised by how quickly it dried, she suggested to Logan that she could wash her hair onstage. Oscar immediately came up with the number "I'm Gonna Wash That Man Right Outa My Hair." The novelty of the scene inspired the team to work out inventive details. Martin would sing in a jerry-built shower suggested by Michener's story "Dry Rot." She would flick suds at her entourage of nurses while she sang, and then towel off her hair. It became a brilliant addition to the onstage antics.

Other modifications followed. The primary ones involved Pinza's character Emile and William Talbert's Joe Cable. At first Pinza stumbled in his diction, pronouncing the word "enchanted" as "enchonted." His major challenge throughout the rehearsals was overcoming his operatic discipline and easing himself into the character and voice of a South Pacific French planter. Rodgers and Hammerstein had provided Pinza with a song for the final act called "Now Is the Time," to be sung before Emile and Cable head into enemy territory. Oscar's lyrics ran "Now is the time to act, no other time will do." But during staging discussions, Josh maintained that they could not be standing and singing when they should be, as the song suggested, taking action. The team met in emergency session. They decided that the lyrics must be a lament over losing Nellie, not a song about an impending battle. Rodgers asked for a brief title from which to work. Oscar called out, "This nearly was mine." Rodgers hummed the words. "That's it. A big bass waltz." Working quickly, the pair brought the song "This Nearly Was Mine" to Pinza, who loved its soaring, heartfelt lines and rich, mournful music.

The team also thought a song was needed for Cable after his lovemaking with Liat in the hut. Studying the scene, Hammerstein became fascinated with Liat's devotion to Cable as she waits for his boat to come into view. Oscar penned the lyrics "My friend, my friend / Is coming around the bend." When Josh heard these words, he blurted, "That's awful! That's the worst song I ever heard. Good God, that's terrible!" After absorbing the shock, Oscar and Dick came up with a new song that began "Suddenly lucky / Suddenly our arms are lucky." Josh was, again, not impressed. "I love the tune," he said, "but isn't that song a bit lightweight for a hot, lusty boy to sing right after making love to a girl who will change his life?"

Rodgers, testily announcing that he was not going to write song after song to please Josh, dredged up a number called "My Wife" that the team had dropped from *Allegro*. Oscar took the song back to his apartment, wrote fresh lyrics for it, and returned with "Younger Than Springtime," which became both a showstopper in the musical and a classic afterwards.

The show's weeklong trial in New Haven was followed by another in Boston, where it continued to enthrall crowds. Before it left Connecticut, one prominent theatergoer, Mike Todd, mock-implored: "Don't take it to New York. It's too good for them. It's too goddamn good for New York." Boston critic Elliot Norton wrote that his only regret was that it was "impossible in a small space to do more than hint at all the wonders of *South Pacific*." Fellow reviewer Elinor Hughes began her column: "Everyone knows it's dangerous to expect too much from any show, even a Rodgers and Hammerstein musical, but whatever anyone expected from *South Pacific*, which tore the lid off the Shubert Theatre last night, it fell short of what actually took place." The show, she said, was "South Terrific, and then some!"

Two days before the trumpeted New York premiere, Hammerstein called Michener and offered him a sweetheart deal. In addition to his initial 1 percent royalty as author—a pittance by comparison—R&H would cut him in on the projected success of *South Pacific* as an investor. For only $4,500 he could buy 6 percent of the property. At the moment, Michener and Vange were building a custom home in Pipersville, just north of Doylestown, and he had to admit he did not have the money. Hammerstein offered to float him a loan until royalties started accruing. An astonished Michener hung up the phone and plopped into a chair.

Without knowing it, he had begun the process of becoming an independent writer and securing his financial future. Two days later *South Pacific* started its incredible run of nearly 2,000 Broadway performances. And that was just the beginning. European and worldwide success followed, and with every performance a portion filtered into Michener's bank account. He was perhaps the first and only American author to have acquired great wealth based on a slim collection of short stories.

Two hours before the curtain rose at the Majestic Theatre on April 7, 1949, electricity sizzled along Forty-fourth Street. Customers were lined up, eagerly awaiting the most anticipated musical in several seasons. Tickets were so hard to get that many interested theatergoers had to wait months. Michener and his wife arrived by cab and had to fight through a crowd. As a photographer aimed his camera at them, Michener flashed an edgy grin and gave him a quick thumbs-up.

Josh Logan was at the theater all afternoon, marshalling his forces for a successful invasion of Manhattan Island: to the rehearsal strains of "Bali Ha'i" and "A Wonderful Guy," young men in grass skirts and coconut brassieres practiced their scenes; backstage, Myron McCormick as Luther Billis received his stomach "tattoo," a three-masted schooner that, when he flexed his belly muscles, appeared to sail the waves; dozens of Seabees stripped to the waist and got their dogtags; and farther backstage the wardrobe ladies ripped and soiled Ezio Pinza's fatigues so that in the final scenes they looked battle-worn. While controlled madness descended on the warm-up ceremonies, Mary Martin stayed safely in the ladies' room, poised quietly on a toilet, reviewing her lines. The opening night guest list included a who's who of Broadway and Hollywood, including Irving Berlin, Jack Benny, Henry Fonda, Katharine Hepburn, David O. Selznick, and George S. Kaufman. Rodgers, Hammerstein, and Logan doled out selected tickets carefully; Stephen Sondheim and Harold Prince were included in their exclusive batch. Prince, who later would direct such hits as *Cabaret*, *Sweeney Todd*, and *The Phantom of the Opera*, wrote: "*South Pacific* was and remains the most romantic musical I have ever seen. When the first notes of 'Some Enchanted Evening' were heard—for the first time—you could feel a palpable shiver of pleasure, a collective wistful sigh, from the audience. When Ezio Pinza brought the song to its quiet (and oh so theatrical) finale, the audience went wild."

Michener, stunned by the performance, praised Rodgers, Hammerstein, and Logan for putting the material into fighting trim. "I have never resented a penny paid to others for the work they did on my stories," he observed, "for they knew the secrets required for transmuting words into images that I did not. In *South Pacific* the conversion was miraculous." Jim remained "bitterly envious" that he had not placed Luther Billis, rather than Bus Adams, in the life raft requiring a $600,000 rescue at sea. His one minor complaint was the replacement of Emile's four young daughters with a boy and a girl. "Somehow—and this may be a crazy idea—I think the character of de Becque stands more clearly defined when surrounded by daughters."

A score of critics, ready to praise or pounce, were in attendance. Some of them did not wait for the curtain to drop before racing to the telephone or the typewriter and making their reviews known. Brooks Atkinson of the *New York Times* declared that the show was "magnificent . . . as lively, warm, fresh and beautiful as we all hoped it would be." *Variety* remarked that "Rodgers and Hammerstein have not only done it again—they've topped themselves." Just about every major daily newspaper praised the production. Martin was singled out for the performance of her career, and Pinza became a Broadway icon. In a few short weeks *South Pacific* was on its way to returning its initial investment and becoming the smash musical that people had predicted.

Richard Rodgers was quick to pass along his gratitude. In a cordial note he told Michener: "Anytime I was faced with a very real crisis of having to have you hear the material, I found you so receptive, enthusiastic, and understanding, that the next time it became a little easier until eventually it became clear that Michener was going to like it. I can't tell you what this has meant to me but we have participated in a tremendous success and event that will surely make theatrical history. It is something for all of us to be proud of and you, as the originator of the whole deal, should and must be proudest. I know that I am of you."

As the show continued to draw enthusiastic crowds, Michener was admitted by the stage door of the Majestic Theatre to watch the production from backstage. "It was thrilling to watch the actors," he wrote, "first as ordinary people . . . who were clearing their throats and blowing their noses, and then as make-believe characters onstage in the glare of thirty spotlights. The transformation was magical, and I never tired of seeing how personalities changed in that transition."

Just before showtime, as Pinza waited in the wings, Michener would talk to him about bicycle racing in Italy. Pinza was a master of shuffling between roles. One minute he could be talking about Italian food, the next he would be striding onstage already in character. Mary Martin, on the other hand, remained in her dressing room or the bathroom, preparing herself emotionally for the role, until her name was called. "Two great artists," noted Michener, "two radically different personalities, two attitudes toward art that were worlds apart, but each appropriate to the person in question."

Along with Pinza and Martin, Michener gained celebrity status. At a luncheon honoring the *South Pacific* production team, he paraphrased Lord Byron's well-known words on publication of *Childe Harold's Pilgrimage*: "I went to bed an unknown and woke to find Ezio Pinza famous."

Within a few months, *South Pacific* mania swept America. To meet the public demand for all things tropical, a corporation, South Pacific Enterprises, was formed. There were *South Pacific* lipsticks, neckties, scarves, and even false souvenir ticket stubs that could be left innocently on coffee tables as status symbols. The music from the show was played constantly on the radio, and the album recorded by the original cast became the number one seller of the 1940s.

Swelling its popularity even more, *South Pacific* began its unprecedented collection of awards. The show garnered Tony Awards in 1950 in the categories of Best Musical, Best Director, Best Score, Best Libretto, and Best Producers. It captured all four Tony acting awards: Ezio Pinza and Mary Martin for leading performers and Myron McCormick and Juanita Hall for supporting performers. In Tony Award history no other show, dramatic or musical, has dominated those four categories.

And the crowning glory still remained in the offing. On May 2, 1950, it was announced that *South Pacific* had won the Pulitzer Prize for drama. The Advisory Board cited the work of Rodgers, Hammerstein, and Logan in their language accompanying the prize. A musical winning the Pulitzer was extraordinary. Names associated with the drama award might include Tennessee Williams, Arthur Miller, and Thornton Wilder, but not Rodgers, Hammerstein, and Logan. True, *Oklahoma!* had been given a special Pulitzer, but that show did not compete in the drama category. In addition, this was the first and only time a literary property was honored twice with a Pulitzer Prize, once for the original book and again for the musical adaptation.

There were countless requests for benefit performances, including one for servicemen who had died in the South Pacific, but Rodgers and Hammerstein maintained firmly that no charity shows would be forthcoming. Instead, while performances of *South Pacific* continued to sell out in New York, they formed two road companies, one for an international tour opening in London, the other for a 118-city national tour. The clamor for tickets at the first stop, in Cleveland, was so overwhelming—250,000 requests for the 48,000 available seats—that the theater had to close for three weeks to handle the mail.

•

During *South Pacific's* extensive coverage by the national and international media, James Michener reveled in his good fortune. *The Fires of Spring* was out, and though it was attacked by the press, the public was thoroughly enjoying it. He was working diligently at Macmillan, with one eye on his increasing bank account and the other on his agent Helen Strauss. He was in truth waiting for her to confirm to him that he had the talent and potential to make it as a freelance writer. This happened in the summer of 1949, when all the stars seemed to be aligning in his favor.

One day at Sardi's she outlined her thoughts on his immediate future as a writer. She stressed that nonfiction was more lucrative than fiction, and she asked whether he would be willing to return to the South Pacific to do a series of articles for a major travel magazine. Jim looked at her mystified. Would any magazine pay to send him there? he wondered.

With a few days Strauss had negotiated a deal with *Holiday* magazine for a series of articles about the South Pacific to be written by the Pulitzer Prize–winning author of *Tales of the South Pacific*. With the public imagination ignited by the musical, a series of articles about the tropics was a natural fit. She persuaded the editors to send Michener on a four-month, all-expense-paid trip. After she telephoned Michener and got his wholehearted assent, she marched over to Random House, where she secured an agreement to publish Michener's articles in book form after the series appeared in *Holiday*.

By June the contracts were signed, and with the backing of his friends and agent—not to mention the windfall proceeds about to be delivered from *South Pacific*—Michener resigned from Macmillan. For the first time in nearly fifteen years, he did not have a daily job at which to report.

In early August 1949 Jim and Vange boarded a plane for San Francisco, where they would lay over for the flight to Honolulu and thence to points around the South Pacific. Their itinerary included sojourns in Tahiti, Bora Bora, the Marquesas, Rarotonga, Fiji, Samoa, Guadalcanal, New Guinea, Espíritu Santo, New Zealand, and Australia. In many ways Jim was jaded by the hubbub surrounding *Tales* and the musical. It seemed that one of the few places not affected by the fever was, well, the South Pacific.

PART III

Return to Paradise

Island Hopping

By the mid-twentieth century, larger, faster, more fuel-efficient planes had made international air travel accessible to the average citizen. Most Americans, however, still considered Europe the prime destination; Asia and the Pacific remained out of the picture and were regarded by many as backward, primitive, repressive, and incapable of forming democracies in which justice and capitalism could flourish. This ill-conceived perception of Asia and the Pacific islands helped Michener establish his career.

Before leaving America, Jim had lectured at Washington and Lee University in Virginia, where he discussed his writing life. Afterward a student commented that it must be easy for him to write because he had traveled so much. Jim responded that it was not his intention to write about foreign lands but to focus on American culture. "The writer's job," he said, "is to dig down where he is. He must write about the solid, simple things of his own land."

When the *Holiday* assignment came along, he reneged on this commitment and grasped the opportunity to educate America about the wonders and opportunities of the Pacific world. Although he still believed strongly in writing about his own country, he recognized that Asia and the South Pacific, if not understood properly, posed an economic threat to the United States. "If we are not intelligent," he cautioned, "or if we cannot cultivate understanding in Asia, then the traffic will be armed planes, battleships, submarines and death. In either alternative we may be absolutely certain that from now on the Pacific traffic will be a two-way affair." He warned that Asia would replace Europe as the major player, and that it was foolish to consider "the South Pacific as a lecher's paradise or a wastrel's retreat."

And so in the end, he looked upon his South Pacific adventure more as an obligation to educate Americans than as a paid vacation. Yet he did not wish to simply rehash the work of Stevenson, Melville, Maugham, or James Norman Hall—or, frankly, his own. Seeking a fresh approach, he alighted upon a novel idea. He would write an extensive article on a place, and then follow it up with a fictional piece, its ideas generated by the themes of the essay, so that "the reader could see from the essay what I thought about a given island; while from the fictional story he could determine what the island thought about itself." As far as Michener knew, this type of book had never been written.

One by one, he visited the islands that had meant so much to him during the war. He reunited with old friends and wartime comrades, some of whom had stayed on after the military departed the region. He met beachcombers, ex-coastwatchers, bar owners, and the normal bits of human wreckage that seemed to wash up on the beaches of paradise.

He rediscovered the plethora of atolls that dot the ocean and in their remoteness found abundant and nourishing life. In many ways, James Michener was a human atoll: he never knew who his biological parents were; his siblings were all foster children who came and went in the household where he grew up; his second marriage was about to dissolve because of his incessant wanderings; and his two adopted children would become estranged from him. Always fed by his writing life, perpetually kept alive by his next assignment, he moved through life an island unto himself.

On the atolls of Polynesia, on these tongues of sand studded with coconut palms, Jim found refreshment and peace.

Lost in a wilderness of ocean, the atoll is a haven that captivates the mind and rests the human spirit.

More than a symbol, however, the atoll is a reservoir of tangible beauty. Fleecy clouds hang over it, so that in the dawn it wears a flaming crest of gold. At midday it seems to dream in the baking heat, its colors uncompromisingly brilliant. At sunset the clouds once more reflect a shimmering brilliance. At night stars seem to hover just out of reach, and if there is a moon it does not dance upon the waters. Its reflection lies there passively like a silvered causeway to the opposite shore.

But Michener was willing to admit that atolls have attracted the attention of misguided souls and moon-besotted novelists.

> Much romantic nonsense has been written about atolls. Even the word lagoon has been debased far below its true currency. On the motus [islets] the beautiful girls have been ridiculed; the patient native men have been burlesqued. A thousand wastrels have befouled the islands; a hundred sentimentalists have defamed them.
> ... To say that men have died in such places, engulfed in disillusion and despair, is merely to point out that on a lonely atoll, as in most cities, good men find loveliness, weak men find evil.

Those islands of the South Pacific generally unaffected by the war—Tahiti, Bora Bora, Moorea, the Marquesas, the Cook Islands, Samoa, Fiji, and Tonga—remained places where he could indulge his romantic obsession for isolation and freedom. But those islands that were torn by conflict in the Pacific—New Guinea, Guadalcanal, and Espíritu Santo—became hallowed places of honor and veneration. He knew many men who lost their lives on these islands, and a return to them was a pilgrimage.

Of the islands that were spared, Tahiti was the archetypal object of man's search for complete paradise. In addition to being "beautiful" and "one of the most fortunate of islands," Tahiti was "a wacky place" and possessed a "unique sexual freedom." Many people claimed that there was an erotic mist hanging over Tahiti, as throughout history the island has lured mariners from around the world.

As a youth, Michener had been intrigued by a cryptic phrase he repeatedly saw in books about early navigators: "so we put into Tahiti to refresh the men." The phrase gave him endless amusement. One chronicler completed the sentence by adding "with limes and otherwise." But the idea that Tahiti, especially its capital Papeete, was a sexual magnet, reinforced by countless conversations among mariners, soldiers of fortune, and vagabonds, continued into the twentieth century, so that by 1949 Papeete had become a rude collection of shanties, opium dens, honkytonk bars, gambling casinos, and brothels. Despite its squalor, Michener maintained a special affection for the place.

He particularly liked strolling through the teeming streets and being acknowledged as the author of *Tales of the South Pacific*. Mostly, however, he enjoyed sipping a cold beer and not being badgered, as he was in New York, for free tickets to *South Pacific*.

By Michener's arrival, Tahiti had a long established reputation as the pleasure garden of the Pacific. In 1768, Louis-Antoine de Bougainville anchored in the islands on his journey of circumnavigation, recorded in 1771 in *Voyage Around the World*. Rousseau and Diderot in France both loved the book, as did James Boswell and Samuel Johnson in England. When Boswell raised the idea of travel to Tahiti, Dr. Johnson replied, "Don't bother, one set of savages is like another." Bougainville had found what he believed to be the new Cythera, a group of islands worthy of Venus, the goddess of love, herself. If Europe was an intestinal knot of political rivalries, frequent wars, and rampant disease, crime, and poverty, here was a blessed land where mankind could reach its ultimate potential. And here certainly was the best demonstration that the noble savage lived in complete harmony with nature. The air was salubrious, the people happy and fun loving, the land as bountiful as any place in Europe or America.

A few years after Bougainville, Captain James Cook, flying the Union Jack, arrived in Tahiti and was scandalized by the sexual practices of the natives. "There is a scale of dissolute sensuality which these people have ascended," noted Cook, "wholly unknown to every other nation whose manners have been recorded from the beginning of the world to the present hour, and which no imagination could possibly conceive."

By 1850, and after the success of Melville's *Omoo*, the word went out: Tahiti was *the* place to be in the Pacific. Stevenson actually preferred Tahiti to Samoa. A year after Stevenson settled in Samoa in 1890, Paul Gauguin arrived by steamship in Papeete, hoping to break the shackles of civilization and forge a new direction in his painting. He headed for Tahiti's south coast, where he began his breakthrough series of Polynesian landscapes and portraits of women. After growing disenchanted with Tahitian life, racked by syphilis and opium addiction, he left for the island of Hiva Oa in the Marquesas. Lacking most of the essentials of a painter, Gauguin nevertheless worked tirelessly at his art, often relinquishing painting for a turn at wood carving and sculpture. The authorities in the nearby town of Atuona despised him and wished to rid themselves of what they considered a savage and dissolute vagrant.

Gauguin liked to think of himself as a primitive and a savage. He once sculpted a crude bronze self-portrait. In 1903 he wrote: "I am a savage. It's true enough. And civilized people sense the fact. I am a savage in spite of myself." The end finally came a short time after this frank self-analysis. One of the natives found Gauguin stretched out lifeless on his bed. Following local custom, she bit his face to see if there was any life. The body did not stir. They buried him on the slope above the village, not far from his house, later boxing up all his paintings, drawings, and sculptures, which they hoped some infrequent tourist might wish to buy.

Within a decade of his death in 1903, Gauguin's name was among the most celebrated in European art circles. His art epitomized Tahiti and the South Pacific. In February 1917, after spending some time in the Far East and making the required pilgrimage to Stevenson's grave in Samoa, Somerset Maugham arrived in Papeete, ostensibly to research and write about Gauguin's life. Maugham was thirty-nine years old. Since the publication of his novel *Of Human Bondage* in 1915, he was poised to become the most popular writer of his generation. He stayed at the Hotel Tiare, a five-minute walk from the center of town.

Like Michener, Maugham was always purposeful, and upon arriving in Tahiti he began his quest for Gauguin. Maugham met several people who had known the painter personally, and all agreed he drank too much, took morphine, and insulted everyone. They also kicked themselves for ignoring his paintings during his stay in Tahiti, paintings that were now fetching large sums in London and Paris. Maugham was directed to a house thirty miles outside Papeete, on the front door of which Gauguin had once painted a crude portrait of a Tahitian woman with a rabbit and a flowering tree. Maugham asked the owner of the house whether he wished to sell the door. "But I shall have to buy a new door," said the man. "How much will it cost?" asked Maugham. "A hundred francs." "All right," Maugham replied, "I'll give you two hundred." Maugham quickly unscrewed the hinges, carefully placed the door inside his car, and drove back to Papeete. Thus began Maugham's collection of Gauguin's art. The purchase of the door was one of the first stops on his fruitful search for Gauguin's legacy in Tahiti, a search culminating in the 1919 novel *The Moon and Sixpence*.

Michener's association with Gauguin went beyond the mere infatuation of one writer for a great artist. The two shared an adoration of Japanese woodblock prints. Gauguin had studied them carefully in Europe before leaving for the South Seas, his art highly influenced by their design and subject matter. Michener discovered the wonders of Japanese art as a boy; by the time he traveled to the South Pacific in late 1949 he was well on his way to amassing a collection numbering between 4,000 and 5,000 rare prints.

Michener called James Norman Hall, coauthor of the *Bounty* trilogy and several other important works on the South Pacific, "the most loved American who ever came to the tropics. . . . He enjoyed a place in island society such as few writers have known in any society." With his wife Lala, who was part Polynesian, Hall settled down in a rambling wooden house a few miles from the center of Papeete. When the Micheners came to town, Hall invited them to dinner, where he regaled them with tales of Tahiti "the way it used to be." "Not the greatest writer to write about the South Pacific," Michener judged, "he nevertheless wrote some of the greatest books."

From Tahiti and other islands of French Polynesia, the Micheners visited the Cook Islands; from there they headed to Tonga and then on to Samoa and Fiji. Jim gathered information and conducted interviews with local shop owners and government officials. Blending interesting, colorful detail, linguistic oddities, and historical anecdotes with the demographic facts about the islands, he created for the reader a brilliant kaleidoscope of island lore. As readers of *Holiday* later recognized, Michener was as good a nonfiction travel writer as he was a novelist—maybe even better. He combined a strong storytelling sense with a gift for observation. He was a skillful interviewer with an odd technique of taking few notes, relying on his keen memory to recall the interview verbatim. Michener's accounts of postwar Polynesia and Melanesia, before the arrival of jets, cruise ships, hotel chains, and squadrons of tourists, provided many readers of the early 1950s with their first experience of the South Pacific.

•

In Fiji, on the eastern edge of Melanesia, Michener painted a blissful portrait of a tropical Eden:

> Imagine a group of islands blessed by heaven, rich in all things needed to build a good life, plus gold mines and a good climate. Picture a native population carefree, delightful and happy. Add a white government that works overtime to give honest service. Top it all off with a democracy that enables dozens of different levels of society—from Oxford graduates to bush dwellers—to have a fine time. That makes a pretty wonderful colony, doesn't it?
>
> There's only one thing wrong with that picture of Fiji. The Indians. Nobody can stand the Indians.

Michener's assessment of the Indian problem in Fiji was particularly harsh. He never equaled this stern judgment in any of his other writings. He continued:

> It is almost impossible to like the Indians of Fiji. They are suspicious, vengeful, whining, unassimilated, provocative aliens in a land where they have lived for more than seventy years. They hate everyone: black natives, white Englishmen, brown Polynesians and friendly Americans. . . . Above all, they are surly and unpleasant. It is possible for a traveler to spend a week in Fiji without ever seeing an Indian smile.

Why this vicious hatred of the Indians of Fiji? Michener was perhaps most offended by the Indians' refusal to help fight the Japanese during the war. He predicted that one day they would outnumber the native Fijians and become "a colony owned, populated, and governed by Indians."

As Michener suggested, the issue was a relatively new one. In May of 1879 a labor transport ship traveling from Calcutta offloaded 463 indentured servants, who were destined to help the native Melanesians harvest sugarcane. These people from the subcontinent of India were made to sign five-year agreements of servitude, after which they could remain in Fiji and seek work on their own. Living in squalid shacks on the edge of the fields, they soon grew in population, so that by the mid-twentieth century their numbers were nearly equal to the indigenous Fijians. The Indians had a different religion, a different language, and essentially a different culture. Friction between the groups increased, with fierce resentment often exploding into violence. When Michener arrived, the tension between the Indians and the native Fijians was palpable.

Slavery, forced labor, and indentured servitude were ways of life in the South Pacific before the mid-twentieth century; many cultures were formed because of them, including that of Espíritu Santo, and a few were thrown into chaos because of them. Michener considered the possibility that war between Indians and natives in Fiji could ignite revolution throughout the South Pacific and eventually spread to the nearer parts of Asia. Hence he blamed the Indians for upsetting the delicate balance of Fijian culture.

The cultural tension on Fiji became a microcosm of the problem facing the cultures of the South Pacific, and it became Michener's signature issue. In his future works he would deal with the problems of migration and settlement, conflict and harmony in various cultures: In the novel *Hawaii* he would depict how several races—Japanese, Chinese, Polynesians—settled the Islands and how they achieved a harmonious society. In *The Source* he would delve into the centuries-old problems facing Arab and Jew. In *Iberia* he would probe the warring factions in Franco's Spain. And in *The Covenant* he would illustrate the friction between the Dutch and the English, and eventually between the white South Africans and the blacks. In short, the social tension in Fiji heralded a new direction in Michener's career.

•

For many years before the war, the Solomons were dark forbidding islands. Horrified by rumors of cannibalism and massacres, many mariners simply stayed away. In 1907 Jack London sailed to the Solomons as part of his voyage to the South Pacific aboard his private schooner, the *Snark*. Like many others, he remained afraid of them. "If I were a king," London wrote, "the worst punishment I could inflict on my enemies would be to banish them to the Solomons. On second thought, king or no king, I don't think I'd have the heart to do it." But London, always up for a good adventure, could not resist voyaging there. With a crew armed to the teeth with rifles and pistols, he patrolled the coastlines of several islands in his schooner, periodically going ashore and mingling with the natives. There seemed little adventure, however, as he complained of skin sores, fever, and dysentery.

The Solomons stayed remote until World War II, when the Japanese invaded, hoping to secure a permanent foothold in the eastern Pacific on their way to taking New Zealand and Australia. The Americans intervened and fought some ugly, protracted battles for the islands, leaving them with ruined harbors, scarred villages, and blasted terrain. After the war, the Solomons struggled simply to maintain themselves. Tourism, mostly stimulated by the recent war, drew some veterans back to its shores.

The Solomons, however, suffered from name disfigurement. Guadalcanal did not have the melodious ring of a Rarotonga or a Moorea. It was war-torn and blighted, a miserable backwater place that people wanted to forget about. The navy called it simply "Guadal" and left it as a ravaged souvenir of island fighting.

When the Solomon Islands were formally returned to the British after the war, a debate raged over where to locate the capital city. The choices were narrowed to two locations, one being Tulagi and the other some new place that would be built from the ground up. Since Tulagi was damaged by the war and its harbor still in tatters, the logical choice was to create a new capital city, which they did, just to the west of Henderson Field at a spot below Point Cruz.

While rotting carcasses of American jeeps and fighter jets still littered the roadsides nearby, the new capital, called Honiara, was slowly built. Honiara, which means "where the wind blows," became an ideal tropical town complete with new bars and saloons, temporary government offices in grass shacks, and a luxury home community perched on a ridge above the city.

But despite its bold new look, the Solomons could never escape their wartime legacy as the scene of some of the fiercest and most strategic battles of the Pacific. The silent reminders for Michener were everywhere. At Purvis Bay, which now lay empty in the hot sun, the great ships of the fleet used to huddle, ready for action. In Iron Bottom Bay, more than a hundred warships from both sides lay silent in a watery grave. In the seas of The Slot, fishing boats plied the waves where, seven years before, armadas of destroyers and battleships had fought for supremacy and, in the skies above, amid the bursts of dark flak, Wildcats and Zeros had grappled and fallen.

Like Gettysburg and Shiloh, Guadalcanal, located far off the tourist maps, was a shrine to sacrifice. "The fidelity of the Solomon Islanders," wrote Michener, "was unbelievable. Hundreds of Americans live today because these brave savages fished them from the sea, led them through Jap lines and carried them in their canoes to safety." Natives, British coast-watchers, American naval and army personnel, all helped wrest the islands from the Japanese. Inland, few vestiges of the fight remained. "Many of the bridges have collapsed," Jim remarked. 'Quonset huts left in the bush have sometimes been completely covered with vines. . . . The chapel has fallen in, the cemetery is gone, only the white steeple remains." Near Henderson Field, Michener found the spot where he heard so many stories emanating from the war, the Hotel de Gink—which, "after five years of complete abandonment, looks about as clean as it did in its heyday, which isn't saying much."

In *Tales of the South Pacific*, Michener had cautioned: "They will live a long time, these men of the South Pacific. . . . They, like their victories, will be remembered as long as our generation lives. After that, like the men of the Confederacy, they will become strangers. Longer and longer shadows will obscure them, until their Guadalcanal sounds distant on the ear like Shiloh and Valley Forge." Speaking both for his generation and for the next, Michener implored: Remember Guadalcanal.

•

Although Michener never touched down in Australia or New Zealand during the war, he considered the lands at the antipodes a dynamic blend of the grand traditions of Europe and the racy vigor of the South Pacific.

Flying at dusk from Nouméa, New Caledonia, to Sydney, he watched as the vast continent of Australia loomed under him. "Here is a land of untold capacities!" he wrote. "Its deserts are more cruel than the Sahara, yet they abound in mineral wealth. Its people are courageous, yet more than two-thirds of them huddle within twenty miles of the sea, while the dead heart of their continent lies barren."

Australia, he went on, "stands like a bewildered woman, at the schizophrenic moment. She is bedazzled by flattering choices, frightened by oppressive dilemmas. She has no clear idea of what she wants to become."

Since most countries staggered out of the chaos of the Second World War similarly dazed and exhausted, Australia was not unique. In the Pacific region, it had borne the brunt, along with New Zealand, of the Japanese thrust southward, constantly threatened with attack and invasion. Tucked under the islands of the South Pacific, it figured little, geographically speaking, among the world's chief players, the United States, Russia, Great Britain, and the countries of the European mainland. Out of the way, beyond the radar of the Western world, it had slowly grown into a formidable country ready to claim its stake in the world. Always fiercely loyal to England, but looking to America for protection, it was not able by midcentury, militarily and economically, to stand on its own. But its unlimited resources, its desire to educate its people, its gung-ho spirit, and its blissful climate, all contributed to its potential greatness. These were the features Michener saw, and they impressed him deeply.

A few days later in New Zealand, he remarked that it was "probably the most beautiful country on earth." You could go a long way there by praising British royalty, recognizing that New Zealand's two islands, North and South Island, are distinctly different, and not confusing a New Zealander with an Aussie. Michener was quick to learn and apply these rules of etiquette, particularly the third. Calling a New Zealander an Australian would cause his normally dormant volcano to erupt. He would remind you that Australia is 1,400 miles from New Zealand and it takes three days of hard steaming to get there. The two countries have no political connection, except their loyalty to Britain. Further, Australia has thirty times the territory of New Zealand and five times the people. But New Zealanders assert they are better educated, read more books, and have more per-capita wealth.

Similarly, Australians have little concern for New Zealanders, whom they derisively call Pig Islanders, referring to the hogs offloaded by Captain Cook that formed, Aussies claim, "the parent stock from which the present inhabitants have sprung." Like two bare-knuckled and black-eyed brothers, Australians and New Zealanders spar with each other, smear each other's good name—and run to each other's rescue when the need arises.

●

When Michener's travel essays accompanied by their fictional counterparts were published in book form as *Return to Paradise* in 1951, he appended a postscript about what his travels "knocking about islands" had taught him. First, he declared that both men and women found the tropics appealing. "On every island," he noted, "I met some woman who had found a home which was lovelier than she had ever known before." His wife Vange, he said, appreciated the South Pacific even more than he did. "Once in deathly humid Bougainville she wavered, but for the rest of the time she loved the quiet restfulness of the tropics."

Second, he found that the great secret of the South Pacific was its delight in "awesome" nature. "Other things being roughly equal, that man lives most keenly who lives in closest harmony with nature. To be wholly alive a man must know storms, he must feel the ocean as his home or the air as his habitation. He must smell the things of earth, hear the sounds of living things and taste the rich abundance of the soil and sea."

Such affinity with nature, Michener maintained, is gained easily in the South Pacific and is what inspired the great writers—Conrad, Melville, Maugham, Hall, Stevenson. Michener liked pointing out that "the great American novel was not written about New England or Chicago. It was written about a white whale in the South Pacific." For Michener, "This part of the world sharpens the perceptions of a man and brings him closer to an elemental nature. It may sound contradictory, but in the languid tropics one spends more time contemplating those great good things of sound and sight and smell."

Finally, Michener discovered a shift in an important aspect of his life. He at one time "was bowled over by volcanoes. I climbed a full dozen of them, watched them explode at night, listened to their majestic growls as they spit forth ash." But now, his taste for violence perhaps sated by war, he found that volcanoes bored him. "Now what delighted me were the waterfalls, those poetic threads of light leaping through the quiet air and finding rest below. I was weary of gigantic horrors and relished the prospect of peaceful movement to some green haven." He mused that "in his heyday Adolf Hitler would have screamed that I was degenerate. I found that I was all in favor of such degeneracy."

Maintaining that the Pacific world was a highway to our future, Michener closed this particular chapter on his affair with the islands in the sun. He always kept a bag in the corner of his closet, however, stuffed with a typewriter, a change of clothes, and a shaving kit.

CHAPTER 15

The Man from Palau

Throughout the early 1950s Michener shuttled between eastern Pennsylvania and various points in the Pacific. He became a regular client on Pan American's famous Flight 001, which established Clipper service between San Francisco and Tokyo, Hong Kong, and Bangkok, with an intermediate stop in Honolulu. During the Korean War in 1951 and 1952, he served as a war correspondent for *Reader's Digest*, reporting directly from the field and establishing himself as a formidable journalist as well as an author of novels.

Michener had arrived at *Reader's Digest* after an unconventional interview with its founder and president DeWitt Wallace. Wallace had loved *South Pacific*, as had just about everyone in New York and the civilized world. Wallace asked Michener to lunch and entertained him with the idea of an exclusive working relationship with the magazine, an offer that Michener eventually turned down. He wanted to remain free as possible as a writer, but he did accept the *Digest's* offer to go anywhere in the world and write articles of his choosing, all expenses paid. Michener considered Wallace a benevolent father figure; Wallace viewed Michener as one of the great up-and-coming American writers and wanted to capitalize on his name. At one point in the interview Wallace asked: "Mr. Michener, do you have some project that you have a burning desire to write about?" Whereupon Michener politely answered, "Mr. Wallace, I have never had a burning desire to do *anything* in my life."

Michener's comment is revealing—and certainly puzzling to readers aware of his character and prodigious output. But to understand James

Michener, one has to acknowledge that he possessed two distinct selves. One was the responsible, steadfast, self-directed writer, capable of producing mountains of prose on a rigorous schedule. This was the self he frequently showed to the world. But there was a second self that he developed as if to cope with the pressures and hostility of the world. This maverick other self cared little for work and periodically enjoyed kicking a can along a dirt road or aimlessly poking along a railroad track. This was the self that he developed as a youth, the self that enjoyed hitchhiking across the country, traveling to primitive, lawless countries, and, even in his seventies and eighties, maintained a regular subscription to the *Hobo Times*.

·

As Michener pursued his peripatetic lifestyle in the 1950s, he was lured into the anti-Communist hysteria of the times by the inquisition of his friend William Vitarelli, who served as an education administrator on the Micronesian island of Palau. After the war the Caroline and Mariana Islands were placed under the jurisdiction of the United States Department of Interior. Palau, a large island amid a scattering of atolls in the Carolines, was located east of the Philippines and northwest of New Guinea and became a particularly favorable spot for tourism and skin diving. After receiving his doctorate from Columbia University, Vitarelli, with the aid of a supportive letter from Michener, was hired by the government to teach on the island of Palau and was given the official title Deputy Governor of the Western Caroline Islands. Once situated on the island, Vitarelli enjoyed an idyllic lifestyle of teaching, making mahogany furniture, and helping the native Palauans to revitalize their island. He initiated the building of schools and oversaw the educational programs that emerged out of the dark shadows of the war.

These blissful and peaceful years in the South Pacific were brought to a dramatic halt when, in the spring of 1954, Vitarelli was suddenly fired from his job, forfeiting his pension and all future hope of government employment. He was initially not told the exact reason for his dismissal from the Department of the Interior, but it came out that three unnamed accusers had branded him a Communist and therefore a security threat. He was flown out of Palau to Washington, D.C., where he stood before a tribunal hastily called to examine the evidence and weigh the particulars of his indictment.

Michener had known Vitarelli on and off since the 1930s, although their relationship strengthened after the war when Vitarelli suggested he might help the Jim and his wife design and build their house in eastern Pennsylvania. As luck seemed to court Michener, trouble seemed to shadow Vitarelli. Michener and others extricated him from one scheme after another. When Vitarelli left for Palau, Michener thought some responsibility would help Bill settle down at last into a predictable routine.

By 1954 the attacks against suspected subversives and Communists had reached into all layers of American society, with education and the arts bearing a significant share of the investigations. In April, Senate hearings convened during which a host of purported Communist sympathizers were paraded before Congress. In June, just about the time the Vitarelli case was being tried, Senator Joseph McCarthy, who spearheaded most of the investigations, charged that the Central Intelligence Agency had been infiltrated by subversives. No one seemed outside the long reach of McCarthy, as the hysteria called the "Red scare" mounted throughout America.

Into this frantic atmosphere of suspicion and fear, Vitarelli was brought to defend himself against the government's charges. Before he got to Washington, he called his friend Jim Michener and asked him to serve as a character witness. Michener at first hesitated, telling Vitarelli that he would like a few days to think it over. At stake were many things. Michener knew that even friends of suspected subversives could be implicated and sent to jail. Reputations could be destroyed and careers ruined by a slip of the tongue. Added to his concern was that during the 1930s he had innocently attended some Communist rallies in Brussels, and his name had been placed on a mailing list. If the tribunal ever got wind of that, both he and Vitarelli could be incriminated. How could Michener under oath say truthfully that he had never had a connection with the Communist Party? He agonized over Vitarelli's situation for several days, finally telling Bill on the phone that he would be at the hearing.

A few days before the hearing, Vitarelli was allowed to see some of the charges against him, which included the accusations that from 1941 to 1945 he was in "sympathetic association" with the Communist Party, that he concealed from the government his involvement with the party, that he had been registered with the American Labor Party in 1945, that he had purchased copies of the *Daily Worker* and *New Masses*, and that he was "not reliable or trustworthy" in his present occupation with the Department of the Interior. On such slim evidence the government, in particular the Department of the Interior, had labeled him a Communist and considered that his employment might be "contrary to the best interests of the national security."

Michener was the first of four witnesses who supported Vitarelli. The hearing took place on June 22 in one of those drab tribunal rooms, paneled in dark wood and barren of decoration. The government offered no evidence to support its claims. Michener took the oath—which did not jeopardize him in any way—and sat down, while a federal lawyer grilled him on key aspects of Vitarelli's character. "Is he scholarly? . . . A good administrator? . . . Did you consider Dr. Vitarelli as a religious man? . . . Was he an extremist on equality of races?" It became clear from the line of questioning that the government's case had little to do with Vitarelli as a national security risk and more to do with its condemnation of a man for his right to free expression.

During the McCarthy era, however, even hearsay evidence had extraordinary weight—a sign of the hysteria of the times. Michener spent two days defending Vitarelli on the stand against charges that seemed particularly lightweight on the face of it, but in the end Vitarelli's dismissal from government service was upheld. "Vitarelli was found to have been a Communist," Michener wrote, "and was therefore fired forever from government service and left without a penny, but with a wife and five children to support."

For the next few years, Michener supported Vitarelli and his family financially and housed them in his Bucks County home as the lengthy appeals process dragged on. Meanwhile they watched Senator McCarthy's meteoric rise end in a ball of flames. Vilified by the liberal press and finally censured by the Senate in December 1954, McCarthy lost most of his power to root out and punish suspected Communists. He died of acute hepatitis in May 1957 at Bethesda Naval Hospital at the age of forty-eight. He had always been a heavy drinker and had been hospitalized a number of times for alcoholism, so the press hinted, and indeed encouraged the notion, that his drinking bouts had contributed to his death.

By the time of McCarthy's death, most of the irrational atmosphere surrounding the roundup of suspected Communists had subsided. As people who were once condemned for their beliefs tried to resume their careers, courts were overturning many of the rulings made in the early 1950s when the hysteria was at its height. Vitarelli and Michener were beneficiaries of this public and judicial backlash.

Seeking to regain his government position in Palau, Vitarelli mounted a significant legal campaign, which continued into early 1959. On June 1 the United States Supreme Court ruled on his case. Citing several inaccuracies and procedural errors in his firing and trial, the Court, in a narrow vote of 5–4, overturned the decision and reinstated Vitarelli as a government official. Writing for the majority, Associate Justice John Marshall Harlan was especially critical of the methods used to condemn Vitarelli. "It is not an overcharacterization," Harlan wrote, "to say that as the hearing proceeded it developed into a wide-ranging inquisition into this man's educational, social, and political beliefs, encompassing even a question as to whether he was 'a religious man.'"

In October 1959, Vitarelli and his family packed their things and left the Michener household. The following month a single-engine Cessna could be seen heading through the wisps of clouds and descending to the island of Palau. When the plane taxied to a stop on the coral-shell runway, Vitarelli and his wife ambled down the stairs into the glint and sparkle of a South Pacific morning. For the first time in five years, he was a free man.

After the restoration of Vitarelli's career and reputation, Michener reflected on those dark years of hearings and tribunals: "I was proud to testify in behalf of many friends accused of being disloyal to their country, and in the process it occurred to me that the type of life I had led had brought me into contact with an unusual number of men and women who were exploring the frontiers of knowledge. . . . Those were bad times, some of the most shameful we've gone through in my lifetime." He was also aware that he had put himself and his own career in jeopardy, coming close to being "blacklisted and perhaps even sent to jail, for the anger I showed in the Vitarelli case could easily have been directed against the House Un-American Activities Committee and I could have been charged with contempt."

CHAPTER 16

Hawaii Mon Amour

As he celebrated his fiftieth birthday in February 1957, Michener also marked the ten-year anniversary of the publication of *Tales of the South Pacific*, a book he had parlayed into one of the most successful writing careers of the mid-twentieth century. He had good reason to celebrate. In that ten-year span he had written four works of fiction—*Tales*, *The Fires of Spring*, *The Bridges at Toko-Ri*, and *Sayonara*—and four of non-fiction: *Return to Paradise*, *The Voice of Asia*, *The Bridge at Andau*, and *The Floating World*, which was a layman's analysis of Japanese woodblock prints. Acclaimed films were made from both *Sayonara*, starring Marlon Brando and Red Buttons, and *The Bridges at Toko-Ri*, featuring William Holden and Grace Kelly. Michener routinely wrote articles on Asia for the *New York Herald-Tribune* and the *New York Times*. His name had become synonymous with the South Pacific, and as his reputation grew, more offers followed, including one to write several episodes of a new television series called *Adventures in Paradise*.

Jim's personal life had undergone a major change. In 1954, after six years of marriage, he and Vange divorced, and the following year he married Mari Sabusawa, a twenty-five-year-old Japanese-American who, during the war, had been confined along with her family in an internment camp in Colorado. After two failed marriages, Michener was quick to blame the presence of war in his life. "War played havoc with my marriages," he explained. "World War II and then Korea kept me away from home." Michener may have been able to justify his marriage breakups to himself, but the fact remained that his persistent traveling would have caused turmoil in any relationship.

He and Mari settled down in Michener's rambling Pipersville home. Mari brought stability and refinement to Jim's often peripatetic and erratic lifestyle. Although she was well read and interested in literature, she had no literary ambitions. She pampered Jim, answered the telephone, arranged his conferences and interviews, and generally orchestrated an industrious writer's household. Mari and Jim both hated to cook, so the couple often dined out at the local cafeteria.

Mari was also accommodating and diplomatic. She was deeply inquisitive about foreign cultures and adapted to virtually anywhere in the world the couple lived. Jim vowed that his third marriage would not end the way his other two did, so he made sure that Mari traveled with him. Often this meant extended sojourns, sometimes a year and a half, in such places as Israel, Hawaii, or Spain. Mari became in a hit in Michener's home town, and when she was introduced to Jim's aunt Hannah, the older woman was

Michener and Mari Sabusawa after their wedding in 1955. Courtesy Library of Congress.

surprised to discover that Mari was a Democrat in the heavily Republican enclave of eastern Pennsylvania. "Heavens," said Mari good-naturedly, "haven't you ever known a Democrat?" Hannah replied, "I think there used to be one on the edge of town."

Jim's and Mari's personalities could not have been more different. She was warm and outgoing; he was as cold as a refrigerator, warming up only to the closest friends and family. At a party, their differences became glaring. At eleven sharp Jim said his goodbyes and waited in the car for Mari to disentangle herself from the other guests on the front porch. "Some of the greatest thoughts I've ever had," Jim noted, "have come to me at eleven-twenty at night sitting alone in a cold dark car while my wife stands in the doorway saying goodbye." Once, when Mari finally opened the car door, she asked brightly, "Did you say goodbye to our hostess?"

"Forty-two minutes ago, and I have a smashing idea for that article on European fiction."

•

After *South Pacific*'s spectacular run on Broadway ended in 1954, it played in other productions, on other stages, and on other continents throughout the twentieth century, finally culminating in a lavish revival at the Vivian Beaumont Theater of Lincoln Center that opened on April 3, 2008. Showered with awards, lauded by critics and theatergoers alike, the musical became one of the classics of the past century. Some seasoned observers went further in their praise of it. Producer Arthur Hammerstein called *South Pacific* "the greatest musical show that Broadway has ever seen, perfect in every respect." To be sure, he was the uncle and sometime collaborator of Oscar Hammerstein II, and thus perhaps biased. But the tough theater critic John Simon declared, "Many are the knowledgeable and discriminating people for whom Rodgers and Hammerstein's *South Pacific*, brilliantly co-written and staged by Joshua Logan, was the greatest musical of all."

Michener, Logan, Hammerstein, and Rodgers took their various paths to other successes. The enterprising Logan developed his career as producer and director of plays and movies. After surrendering the reins to *South Pacific*, he directed William Inge's *Picnic* in 1953, and in 1956 he directed the film versions of *Picnic* and another Inge play, *Bus Stop*, which featured a bravura performance by Marilyn Monroe. When the word went out that Michener's *Sayonara* was in need of a director, he pretty much demanded the job. Although he tried to patch things up with Rodgers and Hammerstein over the original contract for *South Pacific*, their relationship always teetered on the brink of collapse. In 1956 when Twentieth Century Fox, which had bought the movie rights for $1,250,000, asked Logan to direct *South Pacific* for the screen, he nudged every competitor from the field. After refusing many successful projects in the past, he was not about to lose his grip on one of the greatest achievements of his career.

Logan continued his cordial relationship with Michener, and as the movie version of *South Pacific* went into preproduction, he continually sought the author's advice. During this phase, Hammerstein was in the South Pacific seeking the perfect shooting location for Bali Ha'i and a base for naval operations. He visited several islands, including Espíritu Santo and Fiji, before arriving at his prime choice. "Kauai is the island for us," he told Logan in late 1956. The Hawaiian island seemed to have it all: a sublime climate, perfect light, and a nearby naval base from which to use navy ships and personnel for background filming. As it turned out, the navy was involved in actual war games which could coincide with the Operation Alligator of the storyline. Writer Paul Osborn was hired to enlarge and reconfigure Hammerstein's original libretto, which resulted in a screen version running nearly three hours.

The casting of Nellie Forbush, which involved Rodgers but mainly Logan and Hammerstein, was one of the fiercest competitions in Hollywood history. All the leading actresses of the time were considered, including Elizabeth Taylor, Audrey Hepburn, and Doris Day. Eventually, however, the role went to Mitzi Gaynor, a vivacious twenty-six-year-old star of some forgettable musicals of the early 1950s. Logan put her through several screen tests, and the more she worked in the role, the more he became sold on her. Michener approved of her casting as well; as a matter of fact, of the many that starred in the role, Gaynor was his favorite Nellie Forbush.

Gaynor proved to be not only photogenic but talented. Apart from Ray Walston, who played Luther Billis, and France Nuyen, in the role of Liat, Gaynor was the only lead player to sing her own songs. Rossano Brazzi, whose voice was dubbed by opera singer Giorgio Tozzi, was cast alongside Gaynor as Emile. Of all the performers, Brazzi had the most difficulty with his role, frequently stumbling when trying to lip-synch to Tozzi's playback during filming. As the cameras rolled, he became so frustrated that he roared to Logan: "Diss goddamn cheap shit voice, I cannot sing to it!" Logan, who frequently went shirtless on the set and wore a large floppy straw hat to ward off the sun, graciously explained to Brazzi that Fox was spending an enormous amount on the production and it would behoove him to finish it as professionally as possible. Logan's magic seemed to work, as none of Brazzi's temper was evident in the film.

Brazzi, as it turned out, had much in common with the character he portrayed on screen. Emile had fled Europe after murdering a fascist-like bully; Brazzi's mother and father were both killed by fascists in Italy. De Becque becomes involved in a covert operation; Brazzi was once arrested in an arms-smuggling incident.

The musical arrangements, the most ambitious in screen history, were supervised by the acclaimed film composer and arranger Alfred Newman. Employing a 125-piece orchestra, Newman directed a complex score involving main songs, themes, dances, and reprises. The movie featured fifty separate musical interludes, twice the customary number. "The Boar's Tooth Ceremony" was newly written for the film, which also featured the restoration of "My Girl Back Home," a ballad sung by Lieutenant Cable and cut from the original stage version to reduce the performance length.

Released in March of 1958, Logan's movie of *South Pacific* was a near-faithful version of the original stage production, an accomplishment that pleased the director and James Michener. Despite Logan's infamous use of colored filters to enhance certain scenes and his inability to capitalize more on his ensemble episodes, the movie proved to be a box office bonanza. *South Pacific* raked in $17,000,000 in America and even more when it appeared in England. For some reason the British went crazy for *South Pacific*, and it became the highest grossing picture in the United Kingdom up to that time.

·

When Michener visited the Kauai set in mid-1957, he had a secondary purpose. For several years he had been considering a big, muscular novel about Hawaii, a novel that would require meticulous research and all of his storytelling expertise to make it successful. Working six to seven hours a day, seven days a week, it would take more than a year to research and write. The novel would have an exhaustive scope, beginning with the islands' volcanic genesis, continuing through their settlement by various peoples, and culminating in the social and cultural issues of the twentieth century. Ultimately, his novel of Hawaii would be a testament to his nearly fifteen-year investigation of Pacific and Asian cultures.

The novel was also timely, as chatter over Hawaii's impending statehood was in the forefront of the news. For many years Michener had been a major advocate for statehood, believing the Hawaiian Islands to be a strategic fortress in the Pacific. Hawaii's harmonious blending of many tongues and races appealed to his egalitarian nature as well. He saw this Pacific melting pot as "unusually representative of America in that it recapitulates the history of our extraordinary nation. Like America, Hawaii was settled entirely from without."

Hawaii's people—Polynesians, Portuguese, Japanese, Chinese, English, Filipinos, and Germans—gave the Islands their special character and their unique conflicts. Michener was impressed by how the Islanders over the centuries achieved social harmony. Pointing to this end, he outlined a story that captured Hawaii on several levels: its geologic beginnings, the coming of the Polynesians, the journey of American missionaries to Hawaii, the arrival of the Chinese in Oahu, the migration of the Japanese to Kauai, and finally the ways their descendants dealt with strife, a world war, and sudden wealth.

In the spring of 1958, as *South Pacific* was released in theaters, Jim and Mari Michener took up temporary residence in a little apartment three blocks from Waikiki Beach. Although he arrived with an impressive writing résumé, not all authors in Hawaii greeted with him with flower leis. One who thought Michener's reputation was largely undeserved was John P. Marquand, the Pulitzer Prize–winning author of *The Late George Apley* and a literary fixture in the Islands. Marquand privately fumed when he heard Michener was in Honolulu to write a book on Hawaii, calling the visiting author a "journalistic show-off" who "with no credentials or literary qualifications to speak of, had appropriated as his fictional bailiwick a whole quarter of the globe." Of course, Hawaii had seen its share of itinerant writers, from Melville to Jack London and Robert Louis Stevenson. Stevenson had offended islanders by defending the heroic Catholic priest Father Damien, who worked with lepers on the island of Molokai. A local Presbyterian minister had openly vilified Father Damien, and Stevenson in turn publicly criticized the minister. When Stevenson left Honolulu, some Hawaiians hoped that cannibals on some other island might make a meal of him. Michener hoped that his sojourn would be more cordial. However, it was not to be.

Michener's working methods while writing *Hawaii* had changed in some respects since his days on Espíritu Santo, but the broad elements remained the same. Instead of laboring at the typewriter from nine till four in the morning, he labored from daybreak till one in the afternoon; instead of a mosquito bomb by his elbow he had a chilled glass of grapefruit juice; in place of photos, his desk was crammed with research books with titles such as *Insects of Hawaii* and *Ancient Tahiti*. He still plunked the typewriter keys with two index fingers, and on a good day he could complete three thousand words. If he hit a roadblock, he loaded up typewriter and books and headed over to the Bishop Museum, which housed an anthropological treasure trove of South Pacific artifacts.

Although Michener consulted many of Hawaii's top scholars during his research, he relied chiefly on the experience of Clarice B. Taylor, a newspaper columnist for the *Honolulu Star-Bulletin*. Taylor advised him on everything from Chinese family names to the birthing procedures of missionary families. "I tried to read his mind," wrote Taylor, "and put into his hands the literature I thought would help him. Since the only good literature on the culture of the peoples of Hawaii is contained in scientific works, I threw these at him by the dozen." Eventually Taylor would sit by Michener's elbow as he typed, coaching him through difficult episodes. Her personal knowledge of Hawaiian culture often eclipsed the sometimes confusing information found in books.

Michener's faux pas was in assuming that his own blend of fact and fiction would be accepted by Hawaiians. In the late 1950s such a literary technique was still in its infancy. Norman Mailer, Irving Stone, Leon Uris, and Michener, to name a few, were just pioneering its use. Hawaiian readers expected a strict adherence to history; to place real characters in fictional, and often embarrassing, situations was a mockery of their culture. In spite of this, Michener pressed on, hoping that his technique would persuade readers that his convictions were sincere.

The chapters were written in the order in which they appear in the novel, with the opening section titled "From the Boundless Deep" requiring the most courage. Devoid of dialogue or even characters, this twenty-page chapter was an audacious gamble at keeping readers' interest while providing them with Hawaii's tempestuous geologic history. Later Michener would call this chapter his finest piece of writing. Today it remains a bravura opening and a testament to the author's skill at giving life to molten rock and raging surf.

The various journeys of migrating Polynesians, Americans, Chinese, and Japanese form the most suspenseful parts of the novel. Lacking both

Michener in Oahu in the 1960s, enjoying the popularity of his epic novel *Hawaii*. Courtesy Library of Congress.

metals and maps, venturesome natives of Bora Bora left behind their island's social conflicts and economic chaos and set out in canoes for Hawaii. Michener always credited the connection between French Polynesia and Hawaii with his interest in Hawaiian culture. "If Bora Bora is the conceptual germ of my South Pacific books, Hawaii is the flesh and blood. I am deeply entwined with these islands; I hear a lot of talk about their being spoiled. It would require an evil genius four generations to spoil these marvelous rocks."

As it turned out, the nearly five-thousand-mile voyages of the Polynesians to reach Hawaii were minor in comparison to those of the New England missionaries, whose arduous journeys from the East Coast of America trumped most of the long-distance treks of the time. In the early nineteenth century, the missionaries set out from ports like Boston in brigs bound for Honolulu or for Lahaina on Maui. Charting a course that took them south through the Atlantic Ocean, around the tip of South America at Cape Horn, and northwest to Hawaii, the voyage routinely took six months. But few voyages were routine. Howling storms, inebriated skippers, rampant disease, sudden mutinies, and the generally foul conditions on board could extend the trek by fifteen days to a month. And then there was Cape Horn. Usually racked by bad weather, the Horn was every captain's and sailor's worst nightmare.

Setting himself a rigorous schedule, Michener worked at a frenetic pace throughout 1958. Even so, there were diversions. When not at his desk, he might stroll down to Waikiki and blend in with the hordes of tourists. Poking along the beach in a cobalt blue aloha shirt and tan shorts, the sea licking at his ankles, he looked like any other vagabond in this land of expatriates and exiles. He also made a foray into politics. As a reformed Republican, he attempted to bolster interest in Hawaii's growing Democratic Party. He attended fund-raisers and was on hand at a gala reception for the young Massachusetts senator John F. Kennedy, who had presidential aspirations but had not yet announced his candidacy. The senator grabbed Michener's arm and said, "I hoped you would be here. I've always liked your *Fires of Spring*." Was Kennedy truly impressed with Michener's work or was it simply a casual, gracious remark made by a politician? It didn't seem to matter to Michener, as he began to rally behind Kennedy's glitzy bandwagon.

•

In February 1959 Michener finished his 937-page novel and mailed it to Random House, where his editor Albert Erskine eagerly awaited its arrival. Erskine had replaced Saxe Commins in 1954, and he was Michener's, as well as Faulkner's and later Cormac McCarthy's, designated editor. *Hawaii* was immediately placed on Random's fall list and scheduled for November publication.

That summer, as proof copies became available, a firestorm started brewing. Many readers in Hawaii considered that Michener had maligned their history. Originally they had supported his study because they believed he was writing an honest, factual history of the Islands. But when they read that their ancestors engaged in farcical and lewd behavior, they were furious. Lambasted in letters-to-the-editor columns and derided by many Hawaiian officials, Michener made plans to leave Hawaii before publication date.

Not all Hawaiians, however, reacted in anger. The majority, often silent buyers of the book, gave Michener's work enthusiastic support. Most were willing to concede that, although he had stretched the truth of the Islands' history, the overall effect of the work was sincere, comprehensive, and exciting.

On the mainland, *Hawaii* was virtually gobbled up. In its initial months of release, the book shot to the top spot on the *New York Times* fiction list, eventually becoming the number three seller of the year, trailing only *Doctor Zhivago* and *Exodus*. The hardcover edition of *Hawaii* remained on the best-seller lists for nearly two years and retained a spot even after the paperback edition was published. To this day, fifty years after its initial release, Michener's novel sells a brisk five thousand copies a year and remains the premier novel of Hawaii.

Widely acclaimed in the press, *Hawaii* was a natural property for the screen. Helen Strauss sold the film rights for $600,000 (more than $4,000,000 in today's money) and the movie starred Julie Andrews, Max von Sydow, Richard Harris, and Gene Hackman. Although Daniel Taradash was initially signed to write the screenplay by himself, Dalton Trumbo later helped with the script. Trumbo, a member of the Hollywood Ten, had been blacklisted throughout the 1950s because of his reported sympathies for Communist organizations. A top-notch screenwriter, Trumbo brought depth and humanity to the *Hawaii* screenplay.

.

Although the novel's mixed reception in Hawaii troubled Michener, it was discrimination against his wife Mari that eventually drove him back to Pennsylvania. While writing *Hawaii*, Michener had represented the Islands as "a beacon light of hope for all communities who were striving for racial harmony." However, as he was about to return to the mainland in late 1959, a story appeared in the *New York Post* that appeared to condemn his words to the wastebasket. In the article and later in his book titled *Report of the County Chairman*, Michener claimed that "on the day-to-day operating level at which my wife and I had to live, we met with more racial discrimination in Hawaii than we did in eastern Pennsylvania, and my wife understandably preferred to live permanently in the latter place." Michener cited a time when he and Mari were interested in Kahala, an upscale neighborhood in Honolulu, and restrictive covenants against Japanese prevented them from buying a house. He also mentioned that the "three finest clubs in Honolulu admit no Orientals to membership, and other trivial, but irritating, folk customs prevail which a man in his middle years prefers not to bother about." To Hawaiians, who had loved and cajoled their celebrity visitor, it was a shocking broadside. After *Hawaii* was published and it became an instantaneous hit in the Islands, a torrent of venomous letters began pouring in to newspapers. "James Michener made lots of bucks on Hawaii," one ran, "now we're getting lots of his bricks. While he was here, Hawaii was 'great.' Michener counseled us on politics, on city planning, on art. You name it, he was an expert on it." The writer then referred to the *New York Post* article's title "Refugee from Paradise": "Do us a favor, Jim. Keep the title."

The issue dragged on for several years, with Jim and Hawaiians equally insistent about never seeing each other again. But underneath the bitterness, Michener had a great love and respect for the Islands, and even though he might never admit it to himself, Hawaii was still the place that fostered his great love affair with the South Pacific. Hawaiians, too, were willing to forgive as time went on: they could not overlook the amount of revenue generated by Michener's book, and for many it was a more appealing work than a lot of the kitschy stuff in low-budget movies and television of the time.

Back in Pennsylvania, the Micheners made a crusade against racial discrimination a major part of their lives. At one point Michener and his Bucks County neighbors Oscar Hammerstein and Pearl Buck even planned to collaborate on a book about segregation in housing, with each writer furnishing several chapters. Their mission was to author a "short, unhysterical, profound and unequivocal statement concerning America and the race problem." From the outset, however, the book took a polemical and often lecturing tone. Oscar wrote a chapter titled "Dear Believer in White Supremacy," Michener added "Prejudice Is Wrong," and Buck contributed "The Effect of Prejudice on the Individual." Buck spearheaded the attempt to publish their work. Agents and publishers shied away, and it was eventually consigned to Michener's stack of truncated, unpublished manuscripts.

The summer after Michener returned from Hawaii, he was invited to play the role of the Greek professor in an amateur version of *South Pacific* in nearby Lambertville, New Jersey. Sadly, Hammerstein was dying of cancer at the time, peacefully spending his last days at Highland Farm. Jim drove the short distance to see him and found the great librettist and lyricist stretched out on the sofa. Jim took a cup of coffee and sat down, telling Oscar how the show was progressing. Hammerstein regretted that he could not make it to the performance. "I'm sure you'll take it seriously, Jim. Don't burlesque it," Oscar said. "I take everything seriously," Jim said, and chuckled. Then they mused about the early days when many people wanted the song "You've Got to Be Carefully Taught" removed from the musical. "Everyone wrote about it," noted Oscar, "and forgot the love duets."

For several minutes they recalled the times at the Majestic Theater back in the late forties, when tunes from *South Pacific* were on everyone lips. "Those days and nights were golden," Jim said.

Misadventures in Paradise

When Martin Manulis became head of Twentieth Century Fox television in 1958, he was well on the way to becoming one of the great pioneers of the medium. He had produced the hit show *Playhouse 90*, in which he adapted for the small screen the works of Hemingway, Fitzgerald, Odets, and Faulkner. In the mid-1950s television had been dominated by westerns and detective shows, so that by the late decade programming with more exotic locales began to be considered. Series such as *Hawaiian Eye*, which debuted on ABC in September 1959, were typical of this new crop of shows with tropical backdrops.

Manulis had been smitten with *Tales of the South Pacific* and *South Pacific* and wished to bring Michener's celebrity name to television. Manulis approached Helen Strauss in February 1959 with the suggestion that he and Michener create a television series centering on the adventures of a footloose schooner captain who travels the South Pacific ferrying cargo and colorful, often dangerous, passengers. Manulis conceived the idea of calling the show *James A. Michener's Adventures in Paradise*, casting in the title role Gardner McKay as Adam Troy, the lanky, attractive skipper of the *Tiki*, home port Honolulu. Manulis, who like Michener was represented by the William Morris Agency, further coaxed Strauss with lucrative terms.

Strauss liked the concept. She telephoned Michener, who was at his apartment in Waikiki finishing up *Hawaii*, and filled him in on Manulis's offer. Michener would be credited as series creator, would be responsible for writing four of the initial scripts at $3,500 each, would supervise future teleplays, and would have his name as part of the title. He would not have to appear on film. In return, Fox and ABC would receive Michener's heavyweight credentials and the use of his name, which by the late fifties could sell anything that faintly smelled of the tropics. Over the phone, the idea sounded truly appealing. The series was set to debut in October, and the network had requested thirty-nine hourlong episodes to begin filming that summer. Most of the sequences would be shot on the Fox lot in Los Angeles, with additional filming in Hawaii.

Michener had long been attracted by television and had frequently placed story ideas with the William Morris Agency, but none had panned out. In the filming of his stories for the silver screen, he had become accustomed to surrendering creative input to the studio, whose producers preferred to send the original author on his merry way and hire their own writers. He trusted Hollywood producers with his literary properties, and such blind trust got him into trouble with the current project.

After Michener signed the contract with the studio guaranteeing his involvement with the series, he completed work on *Hawaii* and went straight to work on the first script. By June, after laboring for nearly three months, he completed the script, plus a prospectus for the entire series. But dialogue was never one of Michener's strong points, and the script was, for unspecified reasons, never filmed.

In July he delivered the package by ship to Manulis in Los Angeles, who ended up shepherding Michener around the Twentieth Century Fox studios on Pico Boulevard. Michener oversaw the construction of Wheeler's Folly, the lagoon in which Captain Troy anchored his ship. The studio crew also brought in the barkentine *California*, which was dubbed the *Tiki*. Measuring eighty-three feet, the vessel was later used in the filming of *Hawaii*.

The coastal waters of Los Angeles proved to be ideal shooting locations for most of the stock footage of the series. Several films had been shot nearby, including the 1935 movie *Mutiny on the Bounty*, which was filmed off Santa Catalina Island, some thirty miles from the California coast. Viewers didn't seem to notice the substitution of the arid Mediterranean scrub of Catalina Island for the verdant jungle of French Polynesia. Many Errol Flynn and Tyrone Power swashbucklers were also filmed on the coast between San Diego and Los Angeles.

While Michener had creative input for the writing of the series, the bulk of the authorship of the individual programs was left to Twentieth Century Fox's stable of veteran writers, who numbered between twenty-five and thirty. Most of the writers had little familiarity with South Pacific story lines, which added to their discomfort in the early programs of the series. Sixteen directors were employed, to maintain a rigorous schedule of four to five episodes a month. Although most observers agreed that *Adventures* was rushed into production at breakneck speed, few of the studio's producers admitted that shortcuts had been taken.

In September, when Fox felt prepared to preview the series to television critics, they flew some of the most prominent reviewers to Hawaii for a screening of the first episode. Staying at the luxurious Royal Hawaiian Hotel, the critics were treated to a sun-splashed five days while holing up with Manulis and Michener and enjoying all things associated with an adventure in paradise. But Fox's enthusiasm was short-lived, as the reviewers leveled some stiff criticism at the early episodes. Most of it centered on the first entry in the series, titled "The Pit of Silence," which introduced the lead character Adam Troy as the *Tiki* arrived at some un-named Pacific island to collect a famed anthropologist and return him to Samoa.

Written by a studio writer and directed by Paul Stanley, the episode was cited for a host of flaws: poor sound made the dialogue often scratchy and inaudible; the music, which could have elevated the South Pacific theme, was dull and unattractive; the plot was confusing and meandering; and the camera angles were not inventive. While all the critics agreed that Gardner McKay was a future star, the consensus was that the show lacked style and sophistication.

When the critics made their views known, Michener was distressed, referring to the production as a "shambles" and a "catastrophe." Although the quality of future episodes was highly improved, the damage to Michener's reputation was done. In mid-September, nearly a month before the first episode debuted on October 5, he communicated his anger to Helen Strauss. The mishandling of the series, he said, made him look incompetent and only out for the money. "When a story said to have been written by me loomed up with a line like, 'Won't those drums ever cease?' I felt more embarrassed than the critics."

A further embarrassment for Michener was that *Hawaii* was about to be published, and adverse criticism of *Adventures* was bound to hurt sales. A third issue for Jim was that he felt the William Morris Agency and Helen Strauss had, perhaps inadvertently, set him up for failure. A few agency people, Jim discovered, had known that the first episode was weak but did not pass that information on to him. "I spent over a week right next door to the television lot," he wrote to Strauss, "nobody warned me of what the situation was, and I was left fat, dumb and happy to make a fool of myself." In the future, he warned Strauss, he wanted no more package deals.

In the end Michener promised that he would do all possible to make *Adventures in Paradise* a success. As a result, the budget was raised; production values were increased, including the use of accomplished composers and conductors; directors such as Robert Aldrich were brought in to enhance certain episodes; bigger-name stars made cameo appearances. All of these additions made the series a hit with audiences, and it ended up running for three seasons.

Michener's association with the series led to the perception that he had passed from literary writer to popularizer, that he had somehow cheapened his name by lending it to a show with which he seemed to have little connection. The question to him, although never asked directly, seemed deafening: "Why should James Michener, who writes novels, bother with an adventure series on television?" His answer, made public, was simple: "I have had a rollicking good time in the South Pacific . . . it therefore seems to me that the South Pacific is an ideal locale for a television series, and I have had a good deal of fun trying to bring to the screen some of the exuberance of the coral isles I have so deeply enjoyed."

As the television season advanced, it seemed that only literary and entertainment critics mocked Michener about his venture into television. Loyal viewers, unaware of his limited involvement in the series, continued to link him to the South Pacific and to enjoy the show on its own merits.

•

The phenomenal success of *Hawaii* marked the culmination of Michener's first phase of romance with the South Pacific. Although he would return to those sunny isles over the course of his career, he never quite matched the ardor he felt during the years 1944 through 1960. At first, the controversy that *Hawaii* stirred dismayed him; a few years later he was thumping his chest about it. "Almost no book I've ever written was appreciated by anyone in that area," he proclaimed. "I've been kicked around like a football.

The Random House team of (left to right) copy editor Bert (Bertha) Krantz, Michener's editor Albert Erskine, and the famous author, in the 1970s. Courtesy Library of Congress.

But I've lived to see those same people say, well he was a jerk, but at least he was an honest one." Having a book banned in its particular country became a badge of honor for him.

Indeed, as the sixties unfolded, Michener was off on his "genial pilgrimage" around the world, pausing to research, write, and publish a succession of some of the best historical works of the twentieth century. Five of those books—*The Source, Iberia, Kent State, The Covenant,* and *Poland*—became controversial; three—*Iberia, The Covenant,* and *Poland*—were banned in the countries that were the principle subject of the book.

After its publication in 1969, *Iberia* was banned in Franco's Spain because Michener had suggested that the secret religious fraternity Opus Dei had infiltrated all levels of the government. *The Covenant* was temporarily banned in South Africa for its forceful attack on apartheid; later it was "unbanned" by the government because the controversy was actually stimulating book sales. Finally, *Poland* was officially condemned because it threatened the relationship between the communist rulers of Poland and their masters in the Soviet Union.

In 1963 Michener moved to Israel, where he began his two year investigation of the Holy Land, resulting in the monumental novel *The Source.* With *Hawaii* and continuing with *The Source*, Michener's universe suddenly expanded, and with it came his desire to relate the whole history of a people. As he developed the multigenerational historical novel, he refined what he wished to accomplish: "I seem . . . to have had some talent in creating the ambiance in which my stories would be narrated—the look of the land, the feel of the season, the pressure of the atmosphere, the sweep of the ocean, the endlessness of the desert. I have not been afraid of using conventional description and introducing even longer segments of it than most writers do. But I have tried not to allow it to slow down the narrative. . . . I have felt that a man or a society can be fully understood or appreciated only when seen as part of a natural setting."

Moving to a country and telling its story was not an easy undertaking. Some people resented a foreigner relating their own epic struggles, as was the case with *The Source.* But Michener was also quick to remind people that a story needed to be told, and that one might wait forever for a particular writer to come forward to relate it. He saw no difficulty in being the foreign writer to a write the book that would herald the arrival of a native born storyteller.

As his career burgeoned, readers wondered how Michener chose his subjects, which came to be spread out over all the world. "I always carry in the back of my mind six or seven ideas that I am sure will be powerful subjects for books, but upon closer inspection I find that only two or three are really viable," he remarked. Often, however, the idea for a large-scale novel was seized out of the mix by an epiphany: the concept for *The Source* was prompted by an unplanned trip to a Crusader castle

Mari fusses with the best-selling author in 1978. Photo by Russ Kennedy.
Courtesy Library of Congress.

in Haifa in early 1963; *Centennial*, published in 1974, sprang from an idea in 1970 to help celebrate the nation's bicentennial. Ultimately, though, the decision to write about a particular place required diligence and thought. When asked by a group of students how he decided what to write about as his next subject, Michener replied: "Painfully."

Lord Jim

Wherever in the world he happened to be, whatever project he was presently buried in, Michener received cordial invitations with regularity. Mr. Michener, would you be our honored guest at the fortieth anniversary celebration of the battle of Guadalcanal? Mr. Michener, P&O Cruises would like to offer you a guest lectureship on the *Oceania*, sailing from Suva to Papeete with stops in Rangiroa, Bora Bora, and Moorea. Mr. Michener, the government of New Guinea requests your presence . . . He usually put on hold what he was doing, packed his bags, and returned to the land of his first love and the setting of his first book.

These reunions were much more than an aging writer romancing beautiful islands. He made new friends, rediscovered old ones, and witnessed with fervent interest the rise of island groups from colonial and postcolonial outposts to self-governing nations. In 1980 he served as America's ambassador to the ceremonies in Vanuatu, formerly the New Hebrides, marking that island group's emergence as a sovereign nation. Seeing the islands of the Pacific rise from the ashes of the Second World War and achieve independence never failed to make him swell with admiration and pride.

On one occasion he accompanied news anchor Walter Cronkite and humorist Art Buchwald on a good-will journey to French Polynesia. "We toured the gorgeous islands," wrote Michener, "enjoyed native feasts, attended dances held in our honor, met longtime residents with their entertaining stories, paid our respects to the lively widow of James Norman Hall, and climbed the colorful mountains that had been known to Captain

Cook's men and Pierre Loti and Somerset Maugham." Treated like an island god, Michener reveled in these moments in the spotlight.

Hawaii, however, was not all glamour and feasting, as it faced a growing movement by native-born peoples to declare their islands a kingdom, with a full restoration of the royal family whose reign was ended in 1893 when their last queen, Liliuokalani, was deposed so that a republic could be established. Hawaii was annexed by America and became a territory in 1898, due in large part to its sugar industry and its strategic position in the Pacific. As Michener pointed out, it isn't necessary to be a state to be part of the Union. Virginia, Massachusetts, and Pennsylvania are not states, they're commonwealths. When native Hawaiians sought to restore their monarchy, they didn't necessarily wish to secede from the Union (although some did). After the *Hawaii* flap, Michener learned to stay out of island politics, but he thought that a restoration of the monarchy could do little harm and might even boost tourism.

As he approached his eightieth birthday, Michener was richer than most authors, richer even than most sheiks and self-proclaimed tycoons. With a fortune estimated at $120 million, he refused to live an extravagant lifestyle, preferring to plod around in an old pair of khakis and to live in a modest bungalow in the suburbs. His novels invariably rose to the top of the best-seller lists and stayed there for months, even years. His name on a book was recognized throughout the world, which meant, for Random House, he was one of the most bankable American authors. In addition, he had two prestigious art collections, one composed of 4,500 rare Japanese woodblock prints, located in Honolulu, and the second made up of more than 300 modern American paintings, housed at the University of Texas.

Now living in Austin, Texas, he had recently completed work on his thirty-seventh book, another massive epic, *Texas*. With its publication nearing, he showed no signs of slowing down. He kept to the same demanding writing schedule he had developed early in his career. He walked a mile every day, nursing a bad hip. Although not a health fanatic, he nevertheless treated his body with fastidious care and kept his mind stimulated, active, and young.

On a spring day in 1985, the telephone rang and yet another invitation came his way. This time it turned out be one of the most memorable of his later years. On the other end of the line was a producer for CBS television's *Sixty Minutes*, who dangled an attractive story idea in front of him: to return to the South Pacific—principally Espíritu Santo—and relive the high points of his wartime sojourn on the island. As a bonus, Diane Sawyer would personally accompany the film crew and conduct the interviews. Michener had met Diane during Nixon's trip to China in the early 1970s and found her an attractive personality and a competent journalist. After some thoughtful consideration, he accepted the opportunity.

Arriving on Santo, Michener and Sawyer, shadowed by a film crew, visited his old haunts during the war. They stopped by his former quarters at the deserted naval base where, during the oppressive and hushed nights, he had pecked out his stories of the war. He explained to Sawyer how he had brought his stories to his next door neighbor, a man he simply knew as Fred, who had given him the confidence to keep writing. Most of the base was overgrown with jungle. A few miles away, they visited the former plantation of Aubert Ratard, the French planter who inspired so much of *Tales of the South Pacific*. Under new ownership, the plantation was now in ruins. The rows of huts, once occupied by Bloody Mary and the Tonkinese, remained, but they now housed indigenous field workers. Tears came to Michener's eyes as he stood in the silence of the tropical morning, listening to the distant voices of Ratard and his wife as they served roast chicken and good French wine. "Salut, Aubert!" he muttered. "You got me started as a writer." Later Michener discovered that Ratard had moved to Louisiana in 1977 and begun a new life. Bloody Mary had stayed on after the war, but eventually moved to Port Vila, the capital of the New Hebrides.

Farther up the road, deep in the dense jungle, was another plantation, not mentioned by Michener until much later in his life. It belonged to Madame Gardel, a loquacious woman much in the vein of Bloody Mary. When the Americans arrived on Santo in 1942, she set up a makeshift saloon, complete with young women from the island, music, and cold beer. It was a scaled-down version of the Cosmopolitan Club run by Aggie Grey in Samoa, but it served to entertain the troops on Santo. Madame Gardel initiated an agreement with the military, swapping entertainment for generators, gasoline, and anything else that seemed important to her at the time.

Michener and Sawyer found Madame Gardel very much alive, living a meager existence in a grass hut. At ninety-five, she possessed only her dirt floor, a dress, a plate, a knife—nothing else. Her plantation, once the finest in the New Hebrides, had vanished, swallowed by the jungle. After a moment, she recognized Michener and they relived old times. Before leaving, the film crew asked if she could use anything to make her life easier. Madame Gardel thought for a moment and answered: "Mais oui! Une voiture! Une Subaru-267." A new Subaru! Michener recalled her negotiating powers with the American military and how she never asked for anything trivial. Later in Luganville, Michener bought a traveler's check in her name and asked the store's manager to take care of Madame Gardel's immediate needs.

After making some inquiries, the crew eventually tracked down another significant person in Michener's wartime life. Aggie Grey, the gracious and gregarious owner of the Cosmopolitan Club in Apia, spent the hot months away from Samoa in Auckland, New Zealand, where she kept a modest seaside home. The crew and Michener found her there, still bubbly in her late eighties, and still the Queen of the Pacific, as an Australian newspaper had dubbed her.

Michener's reunion with Aggie Grey in Auckland, New Zealand, 1986. Courtesy Library of Congress.

Michener and Aggie had a sentimental reunion, complete with Samoan music and, just for old times' sake, a glass of cold beer. They sang the old songs that use to reverberate through the Cosmopolitan Club during the war: "Samoa Siva-Siva," "Tofa, My Felengi" (Goodbye, My Friend), and "You Are My Chunchine" (Sunshine). Michener singled out Aggie as being instrumental to his beginnings as a writer. "She taught me so much about the South Pacific, because she encouraged me to go to distant islands, and she taught me the songs, the dances, and the customs. Such things are the backbone of writing, and without those days at Aggie's, sitting in the corner and listening, I might have never found the courage to make the big attempt."

•

Four years later, on a bright South Pacific morning, the cruise ship *Wind Song* set sail from the Marquesas for Bora Bora in French Polynesia, leaving the echoes of Melville and Gauguin in the lush valleys of the hinterland. Lazy windjammer clouds banded the sky and sailed in a uniform line to the horizon. Aboard the *Wind Song*, with a crowd gathered around him on deck, was the ship's famous guest James Michener, dressed in a white shirt, blue jacket, and tan trousers, his hands animating his tropical memories. He talked and then answered questions for several minutes, while passengers milled around and handed him their worn copies of *Tales of the South Pacific* and *Return to Paradise* for him to sign.

For Michener, these were precious times when he could emerge from the cocoon of his writing and be with the people who made it all happen. After his lecture and discussion, he could relax on deck and watch the clouds drift along, seeming to pull the whole universe with them. He was flattered to be along on these voyages, partly because he liked being so closely associated with South Pacific culture and partly because it was a way of honoring those men and women, some friends and comrades, who served here during the war. His fellow passengers might have appreciated being with a notable writer in the region he made famous, but he always felt he was on board out of a sense of duty and obligation.

Unknown to Michener, the captain of the *Wind Song* had planned a special surprise reception for him upon arrival in Bora Bora. In the morning Michener was on deck to see the island's great volcano rising into the dawn's light. As they entered the quiet lagoon, eleven ceremonial canoes, each manned by proud half-naked warriors, circled the bow of the ship. From the lead canoe, a noble warrior stood up and bellowed through a bullhorn: "James Michener! Come home to your island!" The ship's staff then led Jim and Mari down the gangway into that canoe, where the couple were greeted with flower leis, music, and cheers from the native men and women. The canoe whisked them to shore, where a hundred or so people were lined up to shake their hands and shower them with frangipani blossoms. "All that day," Michener wrote, "as I moved about the island from one celebration the next, islanders came to tell me: 'You were good to us in uniform but even better in your books. You wrote of us as we are, and the entire island wants to celebrate your return.'"

Forty-five years before, then-Lieutenant Michener first touched down on the airstrip of Bora Bora and saw the dark plug of the dormant volcano, the bright fringes of green surrounding it, and the pale blue lagoon. He called it "the most beautiful island in the world." In the years following, he treated its citizens with dignity and wrote of them with affection. Evidently, the islanders never forgot.

·

One of Michener's most treasured activities during his later years was working with young writers in college and university writing programs. He became so involved with them that he ended up donating vast sums of money to fund and spearhead various MFA programs around the country. The University of Texas, the University of Iowa, and the University of Miami were all recipients of Michener's generosity. More than the money, however, was the personal contact with a roomful of aspiring writers.

During the late 1980s and early 1990s, Michener spent much time in Florida, researching and writing *Caribbean*, and when not chained to his desk or poking through a library, he frequently met with Florida college students to discuss their work and their aspirations in publishing. Such moments were as rewarding as a reunion in Samoa or a celebration in Vanuatu.

On one occasion in early 1993, Michener played "editor" to a group of eighteen budding writers at Eckerd College in St. Petersburg, Florida. Sitting at the head of a long table littered with paper and pens, he placed his hands on a stack of manuscripts that the students had submitted for him to read and comment on. The students' ages ranged from twenty to forty-five. Some had published stories in journals, but most were fledgling writers hoping their carefully double-spaced tomes would someday find a publisher. At eighty-six and with more than forty published books, the master would, they hoped, show them how.

For Michener the often five-hour sessions were serious business. He took the time to read and type his comments for the students, then lead a roundtable discussion of the merits and faults of each submission. Taking a manuscript off the top of the stack, he glanced over his comments. "This is a pretty good story. Literate and well put together. Debbie spent a lot of time on this one."

The student, Debra Macdonald, looked sheepishly at Michener. "What bothers me," Jim continued, rapping a pencil on the corner of the table, "is that near the bottom of the second page we have this terrific episode where a kid is bitten by a snake in the jugular. But it seems thrown away. Not enough buildup. You've got to give it some pizzazz, but don't ask me how." The students broke into laughter, including Debra, who said: "That was going to be my next question." And there was more laughter.

Around the table Michener spread his combination of blunt criticism, qualified praise, and endless enthusiasm. After reviewing the work of four or five students, he paused, pushed the thick-lensed gold-rimmed glasses farther up his nose, and muttered: "You're not a writer until you get in print. Otherwise you're just shadowboxing." After several students confessed that they had "been kicking the same material around for years," he drummed his pencil on the table. "Knuckle down, get it in the best shape possible, and mail it off to someone. I say this as your friend and an old pro. You don't need any more nice words from me. I couldn't have done the work I did in my lifetime just fiddling around and never finishing everything. Do it. Don't dream it."

Next to Jim's elbow stood his venerable typewriter, a kind eclipsed by the computer several years before, and with massive keys large enough to pound with boxing gloves. "I supposed I've done several million words with this beauty," he observed. "They're hard to come by. You know where I find them? I pick them up for twenty-five bucks from banks, where they were put in the basement when the computers took over. I've got nine of them: three here, three in Texas, and three in Maine. I can't risk running out."

Taking another manuscript off the pile, he tried to get back to the business at hand. But he said anyway: "Yeah, you've got to have a good machine to type your stories. A good typewriter and a reliable reader, someone to bounce your ideas off and have him tell you how you're doing with a story. I had both when I was just starting out. It was during the war and I was stationed on this big tropical island in the South Pacific. I had some ideas for stories that I heard on some of the other islands I traveled to, so I sat down one evening and started to type them out. On a typewriter like this one. When I had written several chapters, I got my nerve up and asked an enlisted man who lived next door to my Quonset if he would take a look at them and tell me what he thought. I'll never forget him. His name was Fred. . . ."

•

During his forty-year writing career, Michener fielded many questions about his experiences in the South Pacific. "Did you know the real Bloody Mary?" "Were romantic relationships common between the military and the local people?" "Did you see combat?" "What inspired you to begin your writing career?" The questions were part of any social gathering, and the memories of the romantic South Pacific seemed to lap like the eternal sea on the shores of his daily life.

Like many servicemen, Michener felt a strong kinship with the South Pacific. He constantly reflected on the war years, when in his own mind his "second life" truly began. Such devotion was not entirely his own. Many GI's returned home after the war, took up an old career or started a new one, married, had children, and led fulfilling lives as lawyers, plumbers, or insurance salesmen. Many, however, could not get the South Pacific out of their heads. They returned as seventy- or eighty-year-old men, visited the airstrips that held rickety DC-3s or mangled Hellcats, walked the beaches that they had landed on from LSTs, and pointed to the spots under the coconut palms where their comrades fell or where through God's grace they scrambled up the sand under withering gunfire and crawled into a miserable hole until the shelling stopped.

For many, their hearts and souls were eternally bound to the atolls and islands of Melanesia and Micronesia. Many wished to be buried on the hilltops overlooking Guam and Iwo Jima. Such is devotion. Such is the dedication of those who served and experienced the great, unparalleled drama of war in the Pacific.

Tales of the South Pacific, Michener's small contribution to the conflict, became a classic of World War II, taking its place among other titles from that theater of war, including Norman Mailer's *The Naked and the Dead*, James Jones's *From Here to Eternity*, and Tom Heggen's *Mister Roberts*. But *Tales* is unique among them. Despites its defects, which include a pedestrian style and too many patriotic salutes, it retains the fresh bloom of a stirring debut. No other work of the Pacific war captures the cavalcade of unlikely heroes dealing with intolerable situations and conditions. No other work from the era walks the line between reality and the absurd, between the comic and the tragic, and probes the friction between American and Pacific cultures.

Part of the book's strength comes from Michener's ability to capture the speech patterns and behavior of the Tonkinese and Melanesians. As New Zealand's Maori author Witi Ihimaera observes, "Although *Tales of the South Pacific* is still an outsider's perspective on the region, it's actually closer to the truth. . . . *Tales* is extremely authentic, and the characterizations of the Tonkinese people are realistic, with nice linguistic touches as heard through Michener's ear."

A decade after James Michener's death at the age of ninety in 1997, Broadway decided it was time to mount a full-scale revival of *South Pacific*. It would be the most ambitious restaging of Rodgers and Hammerstein's original musical, one that had a birth at a table at Sardi's by someone claiming the book "had no dramatic possibilities whatsoever." Over the years there had been several minor revivals, and of course the show was a perennial favorite in amateur productions around the world. In 2007 André Bishop, artistic director of Lincoln Center Theater in New York City, began the process of revitalizing *South Pacific* for the modern stage. He wanted to marry the advanced technology of the contemporary theater, the acoustics of a great performance hall, and the lush music of Rodgers and Hammerstein with the intimacy of James Michener's story and characters. He soon assembled a fine production crew, including director Bartlett Sher and set designer Michael Yeargan.

Sher, who assumed the role pioneered by Joshua Logan, began by working out the spatial relationships on the stage. "I am always trying to figure out how the space operates the play," remarked Sher. "The relationship between the language and the music and the space is probably the central muscle of a really innovative interpretation." Sher and Yeargan worked on the mood and color of the island itself. "You have to start with the pure nature of the island," said Sher. "So we start with a very raw and open space. Then an airplane comes in and with it the war. The Americans land and take over." Above all, Sher was mindful of *South Pacific*'s important legacy. "It's almost like a national memory, an expression of survival," he remarked, "and for this reason it is a profoundly resonant show. So there are certain gestures that have to be made—to Rodgers and Hammerstein, to James Michener and to this island way of life—this Bali Ha'i-ness, as we call it."

Of course, the "island way of life" was what started it all: Espíritu

Santo, Guadalcanal, Tahiti, New Caledonia, Bora Bora, Samoa, and a tiny pyramid of volcanic rock known as Aoba. Although most of these islands were central to Michener's development as both a person and an artist, one stood out. Part myth, part reality, part mystical dream, Bali Ha'i clings to the American consciousness. As novelist Witi Ihimaera put it: "For one thing, no matter who we are we must not stop pursuing the freedom to love, hope, desire, and to have something to live for. No matter where we are, there is an island, something that enshrines all that we have desired of our world and our lives—our own special hopes, our own special dreams—where fulfillment exists. It's out there, that special island. We *will* find it. We *must* find it."

Acknowledgments

For this book on James A. Michener, I must again acknowledge the resources of the James A. Michener Special Collection at the University of Northern Colorado and the Library of Congress. I would also like to credit the timely assistance of the James A. Michener Art Museum in Doylestown, Pennsylvania. In addition, I wish to thank some key people who helped shape my view of Michener's life: Richard Gibboney, Gary Pitkin, and Ken Womble of the University of Northern Colorado; Jay Trask, Shirley Soenksen, and Eve Measner of the James A. Michener Special Collection at the University of Northern Colorado; Errol Uys of Boston; John Heckathorn, editor of *Hawai'i* magazine; Larry Maslon of New York University; André Bishop, artistic director of Lincoln Center Theater in New York; Bart Sher, director of the 2008–10 Broadway production of *South Pacific*; Ted Chapin, president of the Rodgers and Hammerstein Organization; Bill Goodwin, author of numerous Frommer guides to the South Pacific; and, as always, the members of the James A. Michener Society. Three UPF people made this a much better book: editor in chief John Byram, project editor Jacqueline Kinghorn Brown, and copy editor Ann Marlowe. For their help I am truly grateful.

Several people suggested the idea for this book, but I would like to single out film producer Steven Smith, with whom I worked on the fiftieth-anniversary edition of Rodgers and Hammerstein's *South Pacific* for Twentieth Century Fox. Steven, quite indirectly, suggested that a story of James Michener's rise to great success would make a fine book and perhaps even a great movie. I took his words more seriously than he took them himself.

In the end, however, it is James Michener I would like to thank. His books have given me numerous hours of enjoyable reading as well an education in foreign cultures. His life of courage and integrity has always inspired me to greater things.

Notes

Chapter 1. The Mutiny

the transport Cape Victory: In his memoir *The World Is My Home* Michener frequently changed the names of real places and real people, and in this case he changed his ship's real name, *Cape Victory*, to *Cape Horn*. Perhaps frightened by lawyers at Random House who warned about possible invasion of privacy, he took the safe route. In most of his accounts, therefore, one cannot be sure that a person's name is entirely accurate.

a seasoned veteran named Lieutenant Richmond: Michener, *The World Is My Home*, 12. Richmond is a fictional name.

"When there's an amphibious landing . . .": Ibid., 18–19.

"I'm to visit all the Navy air units . . .": Ibid., 17.

"Now hear this! . . .": Ibid., 8.

"Lieutenant, is this food as god-awful . . .": Ibid., 12.

"From what I've read . . .": Ibid., 14–15.

"We stood around for a while . . .": Ibid., 16.

"if they were to arrest us . . .": Ibid., 17.

"When a basic principle was involved . . .": Ibid., 21.

"I made up my mind in that poorhouse . . .": Hayes, *James A. Michener*, 14–15.

"Patti was actually a very dear person . . .": Ibid., 51.

"Crossing the line": Sharpe, interview.

Chapter 2. Espíritu Santo

Michener attributed Santo's careful selection . . . : Michener, *Tales of the South Pacific*, 2.

The Seabees of the Third Construction Battalion . . . : Maslon, *The South Pacific Companion*, 30.

Navy censors scrupulously pored . . . : Sharpe, interview.

Fred, who made primitive shell necklaces . . . : Michener, *World*, 297.

"Our war was waiting . . .": Michener, *Tales,* 2.

"Bali-ha'i was an island of the sea . . .": Ibid., 147–48.

He describes the imaginary Vanicoro: Ibid., 147.

"He was in his middle forties . . .": Ibid., 97.

She was, I judge, about fifty-five . . . : Ibid., 139.

"War come. Three years finish . . .": Michener, *World,* 149.

"I would often think of her . . .": Ibid.

Although Ratard was not pleased . . . : Ibid.

"Fo' dolla'!" Mary cooed: Michener, *Tales,* 141.

There was the admiral who . . . : Ibid., 3.

"It was involuntary . . .": John F. Kennedy Library and Museum, "John F. Kennedy and PT109," www.jfklibrary.org.

"Cheerio, Americans. Good hunting, lads!": Michener, *Tales,* 59.

Chapter 3. Nesomaniac

"I was never fond of towns . . .": quoted in Callow, *Louis,* 275.

"I was attuned to islands . . .": Michener, *World,* 140.

Was it "some psychic maladjustment," . . . : Ibid., 122.

"The Maoris, the Marquesans . . .": Lawrence, *Studies in Classic American Literature,* 133.

"Isolate yourself on an island . . .": quoted in Clarke, *Searching for Crusoe,* 89–90.

At last finding a place where "time had ceased to pass": Ibid.

Aggie Grey, the daughter of a Scottish adventurer . . . : Michener, *World,* 37.

"Boy that Tom Collins . . .": Paul Wilson, "The Real Aggie Grey," *Honolulu Star-Bulletin,* January 14, 1977.

"I think half of the good stories . . .": Michener, *World,* 38.

"No one did the siva better than Aggie . . .": Ibid., 37.

Not wishing to jeopardize their relationship . . . : Ibid., 41–42.

"We coasted along the forbidding island . . .": Michener, "The Perfect Teacher."

On 1 December 1941 . . . : Veronica, *The School Island,* 62–63.

"Here was teaching . . .": Michener, "The Perfect Teacher."

This morning I have received . . . : G. Brett to Michener, May 19, 1945, Library of Congress.

Chapter 4. Two Tales

"They tell me . . .": Michener, *World,* 23–24.

"On the remote atoll of Pukapuka . . .": Ibid., 24–25.

"a tough crew of four who had flown . . .": Ibid, 26.

a twenty-year-old navy seaman from Alabama by the name of Gosford: Ibid., 48–50. Gosford is a fictional name. In an unpublished fifteen-page "Confidential Report on Paradise," dated April 6, 1988, and lodged in the James A. Michener Special Collection, University of Northern Colorado (hereafter JAM-UNC), Michener names the seaman as Pritchard on page 4. As the report was not for publication, presumably Pritchard was the real name, and Terua likewise.

"ungodly, subhuman, beastly . . .": Spector, *Eagle Against the Sun*, 408.

KILL, KILL . . .: Theroux, *The Happy Isles of Oceania*, 184.

"the most beautiful island in the world": Michener, *World*, 42.

"I had never met Frisbie . . .": Ibid., 59.

"It was a place of utter loneliness . . .": Ibid., 62.

"We'll save your father . . .": Ibid., 63.

Jim told Frisbie his children would be taken care of . . . : Ibid., 65. Frisbie recovered in the hospital and returned to Penrhyn Atoll to live another five years. He died in 1948 from tetanus, the result of a dirty hypodermic needle. Michener became quite involved in the welfare of the four teenage children. He helped arrange for the three girls to immigrate to the United States; the boy eventually found work in New Zealand. The oldest girl, Johnnie, wrote a fine book of her South Pacific experiences titled *The Frisbies of the South Seas* (Doubleday, 1959). See Michener, *Return to Paradise*, 14; *World*, 64–65.

Chapter 5. Tontouta

only a third saw battle: Spector, 382–83.

"I was always mindful . . .": Michener, *World*, 90.

"What do I want to do . . .": Ibid., 262–64.

"I didn't say, 'I'm going to be a writer,' . . .": Michener to Robert Vavra, March 18, 1972, JAM-UNC.

"No one knows the Pacific better . . .": Michener, *World*, 265.

"Sitting there in the darkness . . .": Ibid., 266.

"One of the evil limitations . . .": Morgan, *Maugham*, 258.

"I wish I could tell you about the South Pacific . . .": Michener, *Tales*, 1.

Jim created a multilayered work . . . : Hayes, 67.

"If I had one purpose . . .": Maslon, 87.

"For whom did I write . . .": Michener, *World*, 266.

"Christ, this stinks": Hayes, 66.

"I cannot express how much I valued his support . . .": Michener, *World*, 267.

"There is a big job to be done . . .": G. Brett to Michener, January 31, 1944, Library of Congress.

"with a contrived return address . . .": Michener, *World*, 279.

Jim's immediate supervisor at Macmillan . . . : Ibid., 268.

"I really had no burning desire to get back home . . .": Ibid., 27.

"Long after I'm dead," joked Michener . . . : Hayes, 69.

"You have imagined your characters indistinctly . . .": H. Latham to Michener, July 7, 1945, Library of Congress.

"We need you and we need you now . . .": G. Brett to Michener, October 8, 1945, Library of Congress.

Chapter 6. *Tales of the South Pacific*

"He could not go back": Lawrence, 136.

"This is not a standard novel . . .": Michener, *About "Centennial,"* 44–45.

"The saddest experience . . .": Michener to Robert Fulton, September 2, 1973, JAM-UNC.

Chapter 7. Coming Home

"the what-it-was-really-like flavor . . .": *Saturday Evening Post*, December 14, 1946.

"You put in words what it was like . . .": quoted in Hayes, 74.

"I don't hate . . .": quoted in May, *Michener*, 72.

"I had talked my way through every school . . .": Logan, *Josh*, 195–96.

"There was a final pilot briefing . . .": Ibid., 202.

"They had blackened faces . . .": Ibid., 203.

"The infantry would be landing . . .": Ibid., 204.

"Who would now want a doddering thirty-seven-year-old . . .": Ibid., 218.

"Josh, the show is falling apart . . .": Ibid., 217.

"Wait a minute," said Hammerstein . . .: Fordin, *Getting to Know Him*, 243.

"His warmth was so apparent . . .": Logan, 220.

Although Oscar was not a musician . . .: Fordin, 191.

"If you start with the right opening . . .": Ibid., 240.

"Don't imitate other people's emotions . . .": Ibid., 241.

Sondheim admits he had a "snotty" attitude: Ibid.

"By the time you get through that . . .": Ibid.

Chapter 8. "An Ugly, Monstrous Book"

"Wartime restrictions . . .": Michener, *World*, 279.

"It enjoyed a faltering life . . .": Maslon, 95.

"isn't going to create a big stir . . .": Hayes, 75.

"truly one of the most remarkable books . . .": David Dempsey, "Atolls of the Sun," *New York Times Book Review*, February 2, 1947.

"a substantial achievement which will make Mr. Michener famous . . .": Orville Prescott, Books of the Times, *New York Times*, February 3, 1947.

"a pleasure as well as an education . . .": quoted in Hayes, 75.

"Michener's trash nauseated me . . .": quoted in Hayes, 76.

"from apathy to tedium . . .": Maslon, 96.

"Mr. Heggen, how did you happen . . .": Logan, 254.

"Streetcar was the best play I had read . . .": Ibid., 238.

"I really love and respect this book . . .": Ibid., 243.

"We would wake her politely . . .": Ibid.

"As brilliant as he was at the typewriter . . .": Ibid., 252.

"Well, it's probably the greatest play . . .": Ibid., 257.

Allegro's simple allegory was crushed . . .: Fordin, 253.

Logan "might glean something . . .": Logan, 261.

"Of course," Hayward agreed: Ibid., 262.

Chapter 9. A Kid from Doylestown

"I can't turn a poor writer into a good one . . .": Michener, *World*, 282.

"my rough childhood . . .": Ibid., 291.

"We couldn't possibly pay you . . .": Ibid.

"Thank you, Mr. Heggen and Mr. Logan . . .": Logan, 269.

"*that* South Pacific *was the bastard child of* Mister Roberts . . .": Leggett, *Ross and Tom*, 417.

"*Submersion in fresh water . . .*": Michener, *World*, 338.

"*Michener, I've been watching you . . .*": Ibid., 456.

"*You have the Dickens feel . . .*": S. Commins to Michener, March 9, 1948, Library of Congress.

"*I have the strong conviction . . .*": Hayes, 79.

Monday, May 3, unfolded like any day in the work week: This was the beginning of Michener's first novel of Colorado, titled *Jefferson*. After writing several pages of the project, he realized he did not have the expertise to bring it off. He put it away in his desk and resurrected the idea twenty years later. The novel eventually became *Centennial*, published in 1974.

"*The need to write is so pressing . . .*": Michener, *World*, 377.

"*My agent had reached the regrettable conclusion . . .*": Ibid., 284.

"*I've told you a score of times . . .*": Ibid., 286.

"*Jim, you've won the Pulitzer Prize!*": Ibid.

Chapter 10. The Prize

"*Congratulations and salutes . . .*": Maslon, 110.

"*Mr. Michener's 'novel' is, in reality, a collection . . .*": Hayes, 81.

"*Only by a liberal stretch . . .*": Stuckey, *The Pulitzer Prize Novels*, 141, 143.

The novel prize was to be awarded . . . : Ibid., 6–7.

By 1934 the wording ran . . . : Ibid., 10.

Beginning in 1934, jurors . . . : Ibid., 13.

"*I gave my reasons for selecting* Tales . . .": Hayes, 82.

"*I liked the book . . .*": Michener, *World*, 342.

"*There was a flurry of interest . . .*": Michener to John P. Hayes, December 15, 1971, quoted in Hayes, 82.

Chapter 11. Mary and Ezio

In musical theater at the time, if two love stories . . . : Fordin, 262.

Because South Pacific *is heavily romantic . . .* : Maslon, 115.

"*I had become restless . . .*": Ibid., 111.

"*He was a kindred soul . . .*": "Ezio Pinza Remembers," in Gargagliano, "South Pacific," 35.

A contract soon followed, stipulating that Pinza . . . : Maslon, 112.

"*As long as we've got Pinza . . .*": Ibid.

"*Oh, the impact of that song!*": "Mary Martin Remembers," in Gargagliano, 34.

"*It was the first time I had been in a purely American show . . .*": "Ezio Pinza Remembers," 35.

Calling it "sententious," "corny," and "sentimental," . . . : Orville Prescott, *Yale Review*, February 6, 1949, 18.

"*I have been damaged, in some ways . . .*": Michener, *World*, 103.

"*brilliant high school stuff . . .*": Hayes, 83.

"*I began to appreciate the great loss . . .*": Michener, *World*, 345.

Chapter 12. Josh and Oscar

"I know absolutely nothing about Army behavior . . .": Logan, 273–74.

"What do sailors do . . .": Ibid., 273.

"I was Billis, I was a Seabee . . .": Ibid., 275.

"You're writing again and you only . . .": Ibid., 277.

"I can only say they have accomplished . . .": Maslon, 116.

"I knew the melody would have to . . .": Ibid., 77.

"It's going to win the Pulitzer . . .": Logan, 277.

"You look strange . . .": Ibid., 278.

"According to our contract, in the credits . . .": Ibid., 279.

"He could have mowed Dick down . . .": Fordin, 275.

"a brilliant, talented, highly intelligent, theatrically sound superbrain": Logan, 282.

"I realize very well the dangers . . .": Maslon, 162.

"I don't idealize people . . .": Fordin, 271.

Chapter 13. Those Enchanted Evenings

The four producers were able to finance the musical . . . : Fordin, 267.

"Mary had landed on Trude's shoulders . . .": Logan, 289.

Martin had gotten a short, gamin haircut . . . : Ibid.

"Now is the time to act, no other time will do": Ibid., 287.

"That's awful! That's the worst song . . .": Ibid., 287–88.

"Don't take it to New York . . .": Fordin, 280.

"impossible in a small space to do more than hint . . .": Ibid., 281.

Hammerstein called Michener and offered him a sweetheart deal: Michener, *World,* 294.

"South Pacific was and remains the most romantic . . .": Maslon, 130.

"I have never resented a penny paid . . .": Ibid.

Brooks Atkinson of the New York Times *declared . . . :* Ibid.

Variety *remarked . . . :* Ibid.

"Anytime I was faced with a very real crisis . . .": Ibid., 132.

"It was thrilling to watch . . .": Michener, *World,* 164.

"Two great artists . . .": Ibid., 165.

"I went to bed an unknown . . .": Maslon, 132.

Within a few months, South Pacific *mania . . . :* Ibid., 153.

its unprecedented collection of awards: Ibid.

they formed two road companies: Ibid., 154.

One day at Sardi's she outlined . . . : Hayes, 87.

She persuaded the editors to send Michener on a four-month, all-expense-paid trip: Strauss, *A Talent for Luck,* 85.

Chapter 14. Island Hopping

"The writer's job . . .": Michener, *Return,* 3.

"If we are not intelligent . . .": Ibid., 436–37.

"the reader could see from the essay what I thought about a given island . . .": Ibid., 4.

Lost in a wilderness of ocean . . . : Ibid., 7.

Much romantic nonsense . . . : Ibid., 18.

"so we put into Tahiti to refresh the men": Ibid., 48.

"Don't bother, one set of savages is like another": quoted in Theroux, 368.

"There is a scale of dissolute sensuality . . .": Ibid.

"I am a savage . . .": Ibid.

"But I shall have to buy a new door": quoted in Morgan, 219. In 1962 the painted door sold for $37,400 at Sotheby's.

"the most loved American who ever came to the tropics . . .": Michener, "Book Notes."

"Imagine a group of islands blessed by heaven . . .": Michener, *Return*, 123.

"a colony owned, populated, and governed by Indians": Ibid., 124.

"If I were a king . . .": quoted in Theroux, 154–55.

"The fidelity of the Solomon Islanders . . .": Michener, *Return*, 185.

"Many of the bridges have collapsed . . .": Ibid., 187.

"They will live a long time . . .": Michener, *Tales*, 3.

"Here is a land of untold capacities! . . .": Michener, *Return*, 322.

"probably the most beautiful country on earth": Ibid., 243.

"the parent stock from which the present inhabitants have sprung": Ibid., 255.

When Michener's travel essays accompanied by their fictional counterparts were published . . . : Ibid., 431.

"the great American novel was not written . . .": Ibid., 432.

"Now what delighted me were the waterfalls . . .": Ibid., 435.

Chapter 15. The Man from Palau

"Mr. Michener, do you have some project . . .": Hayes, 98.

the inquisition of his friend William Vitarelli: U.S. Supreme Court, Vitarelli v. Seaton, 359 U.S. 535 (1959).

"Is he scholarly? . . . A good administrator? . . .": Ibid., footnote 5.

"Vitarelli was found to have been a Communist . . .": Michener, *World*, 245.

"blacklisted and perhaps even sent to jail . . .": Ibid., 247.

Chapter 16. Hawaii Mon Amour

"War played havoc with my marriages . . .": Hayes, 125.

"Heavens," said Mari good-naturedly . . . : Unpublished notes, JAM-UNC.

"Some of the greatest thoughts I've ever had . . .": Ibid.

"the greatest musical show that Broadway has ever seen . . .": Strauss, 79.

"Many are the knowledgeable and discriminating people . . .": Maslon, 130.

"Kauai is the island for us": Maslon, 168.

the navy was involved in actual war games: Maslon, 168.

"Diss goddamn cheap shit voice . . .": May, "James A. Michener's *Hawaii*," 42.

"unusually representative of America . . .": quoted in Hayes, 140.

"journalistic show-off . . .": Birmingham, *The Late John Marquand*, 172–73.

"I tried to read his mind . . .": quoted in Hayes, 143.

"If Bora Bora is the conceptual germ . . .": Sutton, "The Strange Case of James Michener," 21.

"I hoped you would be here . . .": Michener, *Report of the County Chairman*, 1.

"a beacon light of hope . . .": "Michener's Racial Blast," *Honolulu Star-Bulletin*, April 7, 1961.

"on the day-to-day operating level . . .": Michener, *Report*, 8.

"James Michener made lots of bucks on Hawaii . . .": Letters, *New York Post*, June 16, 1961.

"short, unhysterical, profound and unequivocal . . .": Fordin, 335.

"I'm sure you'll take it seriously, Jim . . .": Michener, *World*, 294–95.

Chapter 17. Misadventures in Paradise

"When a story said to have been written by me . . .": Hayes, 159.

"I spent over a week right next door. . . .": Ibid., 160.

"I have had a rollicking good time . . .": Ibid., 161.

"Almost no book . . .": William Bennett, "Michener's Return to Paradise," *Honolulu Star-Bulletin*, November 9, 1988.

"I seem . . . to have had some talent in creating the ambiance . . .": Michener, *World*, 315.

"I always carry in the back of my mind . . .": Ibid., 321.

Chapter 18. Lord Jim

"We toured the gorgeous islands . . .": Michener, *World*, 167.

"Salut, Aubert! . . .": Michener to John Kings, June 6, 1986, JAM-UNC.

"Mais oui! Une voiture! . . .": Unpublished notes, JAM-UNC.

"She taught me so much about the South Pacific . . .": Unpublished notes, JAM-UNC.

"James Michener! Come home to your island!": Michener, *World*, 510.

"This is a pretty good story . . .": John Bartlett, "Writer in Chief," *Greeley Tribune*, April 3, 1993.

"Although Tales of the South Pacific *is still an outsider's perspective . . .*": Ihimaera, "That Special Island," in Gargagliano, 25.

"I am always trying to figure out . . .": "Building a House," interview in Gargagliano, 19.

"For one thing, no matter who we are we must not stop pursuing . . .": Ihimaera, 26.

Bibliography

Birmingham, Stephen. *The Late John Marquand*. Philadelphia: Lippincott, 1972.

Callow, Philip. *Louis: A Life of Robert Louis Stevenson*. Chicago: Ivan R. Dee, 2001.

Clarke, Thurston. *Searching for Crusoe: A Journey among the Last Real Islands*. New York: Ballantine, 2001.

Delbanco, Andrew. *Melville: His World and Work*. New York: Knopf, 2005.

Fordin, Hugh. *Getting to Know Him: A Biography of Oscar Hammerstein II*. New York: Random House, 1977.

Gargagliano, Alexis, ed. "South Pacific." Expanded issue, *Lincoln Center Theater Review*, nos. 45–46 (Spring 2008).

Hayes, John P. *James A. Michener: A Biography*. Indianapolis: Bobbs-Merrill, 1984.

Lawrence, D. H. *Studies in Classic American Literature*. 1923. New York: Viking, 1964.

Leggett, John. *Ross and Tom: Two American Tragedies*. New York: Simon and Schuster, 1974.

Logan, Joshua. *Josh: My Up and Down, In and Out Life*. New York: Delacorte, 1976.

Maslon, Laurence. *The South Pacific Companion*. New York: Simon and Schuster, 2008.

May, Stephen J. "James A. Michener's *Hawaii*—50 Years Later," *Hawai'i*, April 2008, 23–25.

———. *Michener: A Writer's Journey*. Norman: University of Oklahoma Press, 2005.

Michener, James A. *About "Centennial": Some Notes on the Novel*. New York: Random House, 1974.

———. "Book Notes." *Paradise of the Pacific*, August 1953, 98.

———. *A Michener Miscellany: 1950–1970*. New York: Random House, 1973.

———. "The Perfect Teacher." *Coronet*, June 1951, 21–24.

———. *Report of the County Chairman*. New York: Random House, 1961.

———. *Return to Paradise*. New York: Random House, 1951.

———. *Tales of the South Pacific*. New York: Macmillan, 1947.

———. *The World Is My Home*. New York: Random House, 1991.

Morgan, Ted. *Maugham*. New York: Simon and Schuster, 1980.

Sharpe, Marshall, USN (Ret.). Telephone interview with author, June 13, 2009.

Spector, Ronald H. *Eagle Against the Sun: The American War with Japan*. New York: Free Press, 1985.

Steinberg, Rafael. *Island Fighting*. Alexandria, Va.: Time-Life, 1978.

Strauss, Helen M. *A Talent for Luck: An Autobiography*. New York: Random House, 1979.

Stuckey, W. J. *The Pulitzer Prize Novels: A Critical Backward Look*. 2nd ed. Norman: University of Oklahoma Press, 1981.

Sutton, Horace. "The Strange Case of James Michener." *Paradise of the Pacific*, September–October 1963, 21–25.

Theroux, Paul. *The Happy Isles of Oceania*. New York: G. P. Putnam's Sons, 1992.

U.S. Supreme Court. Vitarelli v. Seaton, 359 U.S. 535 (1959). Argued April 1–2, 1959; decided June 1, 1959.

Veronica of the Cross, Sister. *The School Island*. London: SPCK, 1949. anglicanhistory.org/oceania/school_island1949/.

Index

Acushnet (ship), 28
Adventures in Paradise (television series), 144–47
Aldrich, Robert, 147
Allegro (musical), 76–77
Annie Get Your Gun (musical), 66–69, 72, 95
Aoba, 18, 33–35, 160
Atkinson, Brooks, 81, 110
Auden, W. H., 87
Australia, 124–25

Bali Ha'i, 18, 101, 159–60
Bellow, Saul, 89
Benny, Jack, 109
Berlin, Irving, 66, 69, 109
Bill Brown's Health Farm, 103
Bishop, André, 159
Bloody Mary, 20–21, 32, 56, 84, 99, 153
Bora Bora, 37–40, 63, 155–56
Bossard, Captain, 6
Boswell, James, 118
Brace, Gerald Warner, 89
Brando, Marlon, 132
Brandt, Carl, Sr., 79, 82, 85
Brazzi, Rossano, 135–36
Buchwald, Art, 151
Burlingame, x
Burns, John Horne, 81, 90, 96
Buttons, Red, 132

Calhoun, Vice Admiral William (Billy), 36–37
Cape Victory (ship), 3–12, 14
Carousel (musical), 68–69, 72, 99

Caruso, Enrico, 96
Cerf, Bennett, 91
Chamberlain, John, 89
Chambron, Jacques, 79
Clemens, Martin, 24–25
Commins, Saxe, 82–84, 96
Conrad, Joseph, 28, 31, 44, 46, 125
Cook, Captain James, 118
Cournos, John, 74
Cozzens, James Gould, 66, 90
Cronkite, Walter, 151

de Bougainville, Louis-Antoine, 118
Defoe, Daniel, 31
Dempsey, David, 74
DeVoto, Bernard, 87
Diderot, Denis, 118
Doylestown, Pa., 8–9, 65–66, 70
Durrell, Lawrence, 31

Eckerd College, 156–58
Espíritu Santo, 3, 5, 13–25, 159–60; cannibalism in, 17; cargo cults in, 17–18; climate of, 16–17

Fields, Dorothy, 66
Fields, Herbert, 66
Fiji, 120–21
Flynn, Errol, 145
Fonda, Henry, x, 76, 109
Forster, E. M., 90
Frisbie, Robert Dean, 37, 40–44, 84
From Here to Eternity, 158

Gauguin, Paul, 30, 118–19, 155

Gaynor, Mitzi, x, 135

Geismar, Maxwell, 89

George School, Newton, Pa., 9

Gide, André, 90

Grable, Betty, x

Golding, William, 31

Gosford, Seaman, 38–39

Greene, Richard Tobias (Toby), 29

Grey, Aggie, 31–32, 63, 84, 153–55

Guadalcanal, 3, 5, 21–25, 122–23, 160

Guthrie, A. B., 89

Haas, Victor, 87

Hackman, Gene, 141

Hall, James Norman, 30, 40, 44, 116, 120, 125, 151

Halliday, Richard, 95

Halsey, Admiral William F. (Bull), 36, 39

Hammerstein, Arthur, 134

Hammerstein II, Oscar, ix, 66, 68–72, 76, 77, 78, 142–43; and *South Pacific*, 79–112, 134, 159

Harlan, Associate Justice John Marshall, 131

Harris, Richard, 141

Hart, Lorenz, 66

Hawaii. See Michener, James A.

Hayes, Alfred, 81

Hayes, Helen, 69

Hayward, Leland, 75, 76, 77–80

Heggen, Thomas, 74, 76, 80–82, 97, 158

Hepburn, Katharine, 109

Herbert, Victor, 9

Hill School, Pottstown, Pa., 9

Hobo Times, 128

Holden, William, 132

Holiday, 112, 115

Hotel de Gink, Guadalcanal, 21, 63, 123

Hughes, Elinor, 108

Ihimaera, Witi, 159–60

Inge, William, 134

James, Henry, 27

Johnson, Samuel, 118

Jones, James, 158

Kaufman, George S., 109

Kelly, Grace, 132

Kennedy, John F., 23–24, 140

Klopfer, Donald, 91

Krock, Arthur, 89–90

Latham, Harold, 49, 51, 63

Lawrence, D. H., 28–29, 31, 56–57; "The Man Who Loved Islands," 31

Lester, Edwin, 94

Lewis, Sinclair, 88

Logan, Joshua, x, 66–69, 75, 76, 77, 80, 81, 134, 159; and *South Pacific* (movie), 134–36; and *South Pacific* (musical), 78–112, 159

Logan, Nedda, 76, 99–101

London, Jack, 28, 137

Longworth, Alice Roosevelt, 89–90

Loos, Anita, 69

Loti, Pierre, 28, 152

Macdonald, Debra, 157

MacKenna, Kenneth, 77

Mailer, Norman, 138, 158

Majestic Theater, New York City, 109–11

Manulis, Martin, 144–46

Marquand, John P., 137

Martin, Mary, 95–97, 107, 109, 110

Maugham, W. Somerset, 28, 44, 45, 46, 79, 116, 125, 152; influence on Michener, 45–46; in Tahiti, 119–20

McCain, Admiral John S., 13

McKay, Gardner, 144

Melville, Herman, 28, 44, 116, 125, 137, 155; in the Marquesas, 28–31; writing of *Omoo*, 28; *Typee*, 28, 29–30

Mercer, Henry Chapman, 9

Merman, Ethel, 66, 95

Michener, James A.: *Caribbean*, 156; *Centennial*, ix, 150; *Chesapeake*, ix; *The Covenant*, 149; on Espíritu Santo, 13–59; *The Fires of Spring*, 79, 82, 83–85, 96–97, 140; and Robert Dean Frisbie, 40–42; *Hawaii* (movie), 141, 145; *Hawaii* (novel), 122, 132–42, 144–47; *Iberia*, 149; *James A. Michener's Adventures in Paradise* (TV series), 144–47; *Kent State: What Happened and Why*, 149; as naval historian, 49–52; *Poland*, ix, 149; *Return to Paradise*, 125–26, 132, 155; and Samoa, 27–33; *Sayonara*, 134; *The Source*, ix, 149; and the South Pacific, 3–59, 115–26, 151–56, 158–60; *South Pacific* (movie), 134–37; *South Pacific* (musical), 79–97, 104, 106, 109–10, 134, 143, 144; *Tales of the South Pacific*, ix, 39, 44–52, 64, 73–74, 77–78, 80–112, 123, 144, 153, 155, 158–60; *Texas*, 152; Tontouta airstrip, 43–45

Michener, Mabel (mother), 8–9

Michener, Mari Sabusawa (third wife), 40, 132–34, 137–42
Michener, Patty Koon (first wife), xi, 91
Michener, Vange Nord (second wife), 91, 131
Mielziner, Jo, 77, 101
Miller, Arthur, 111
Mister Roberts, 74–75, 77, 80–82
Mitscher, Vice Admiral Mark, 8
Monroe, Marilyn, 134
Morrison, Samuel Eliot, 49
Motley, Willard, 89
Mutiny on the Bounty, 40, 145

Newman, Alfred, 136
New Zealand, 124–25
Nordhoff, Charles, 40
Norton, Elliot, 108

O'Brien, Frederick, 44
Oklahoma!, 68–69, 72, 99
Omoo. See Melville, Herman
Osborn, Paul, 135

Palau, 128, 131
Pinza, Ezio, 94–96, 107, 109, 110–11
Power, Tyrone, 145
Prescott, Orville, 74, 89
Prince, Harold, 109
Pulitzer Prize (fiction), 85–91

Ratard, Aubert, 19–21, 153
Reader's Digest, 127
Reinheimer, Howard, 80, 103
Richmond, Lieutenant, 4–7
Riggs, Lynn, 80
Rittman, Trude, 107
Rodgers, Richard, ix, 66, 68–72, 76–77, 78; and *South Pacific*, 79–112, 134, 159
Roosevelt, Theodore, 89
Rousseau, Jean-Jacques, 118

Saipan, 8
Saturday Evening Post, 73–74
Saturday Review, 97
Sawyer, Diane, 153
Scott, Cecil, 53, 85
Selznick, David O., 109
Shaw, Irwin, 81
Sher, Bartlett, 159

Show Boat (musical), 72
Shubert Theater, 106
Simon, John, 134
Smith, Steven, x
Sondheim, Stephen, 70–72, 109
Sousa, John Philip, 9
South Pacific (movie). *See* Hammerstein II, Oscar; Logan, Joshua; Michener, James A.; Rodgers, Richard
South Pacific (musical). *See* Hammerstein II, Oscar; Logan, Joshua; Michener, James A.; Rodgers, Richard
State Fair (musical), 68
Steinbeck, John, 88
Stevenson, Robert Louis, 26–27, 28, 31, 40, 44, 116, 125, 137
Stone, Irving, 138
Strauss, Helen, 82, 91, 112, 144–46
A Streetcar Named Desire, 75, 77, 87
Stuckey, W. J., 87–88
Swarthmore College, 9

Tahiti, 117–20
Tales of the South Pacific. See Michener, James A.
Tarawa, 7
Tarkington, Booth, 88
Todd, Mike, 108
Trumbo, Dalton, 141
Typee. See Melville, Herman

University of Northern Colorado, 4, 47
Uris, Leon, 138

Verne, Jules, 31
Vidal, Gore, 91
Vivian Beaumont Theater, ix–x, 134
von Sydow, Max, 141

Wallace, DeWitt, 127
Warren, Robert Penn, 88, 90
Waugh, Alec, 28
Wilder, Thornton, 88, 111
Williams, Tennessee, 75, 87, 111
Wilson, Sister Margaret Pears (Mother Margaret), 34–35

Yeargan, Michael, 159

Zanuck, Daryl F., x

A frequent contributor to national magazines and journals, Stephen J. May is the author of the full-length 2005 biography *Michener: A Writer's Journey*, as well as several articles on the best-selling writer. One of the world's recognized authorities on Michener, May helped curate the 2007 retrospective on the author at the James A. Michener Art Museum in Doylestown, Pennsylvania, and is a featured commentator in Twentieth Century Fox's 50th Anniversary Edition of Rodgers and Hammerstein's *South Pacific*. A college professor of American literature and the author of six other books, May lives in Colorado.